World Wisdom

The Library of Perennial Philosophy

The Library of Perennial Philosophy is dedicated to the exposition of the timeless Truth underlying the diverse religions. This Truth, often referred to as the *Sophia Perennis*—or Perennial Wisdom—finds its expression in the revealed Scriptures as well as the writings of the great sages and the artistic creations of the traditional worlds.

A Living Islamic City: Fez and Its Preservation appears as one of our selections in the Sacred Art in Tradition series.

Sacred Art in Tradition

The aim of this series is to underscore the essential role of beauty and its artistic expressions in the Perennial Philosophy. Each volume contains full-color reproductions of masterpieces of traditional art—including painting, sculpture, architecture, and vestimentary art—combined with writings by authorities on each subject. Individual titles focus either on one spiritual tradition or on a central theme that touches upon diverse traditions.

A Living Islamic City

Fez and Its Preservation

فاس

Titus Burckhardt

With photographs and drawings by the author

Edited by

Jean-Louis Michon

&

Joseph A. Fitzgerald

Translated by

Jane Casewit

World Wisdom

A Living Islamic City: Fez and Its Preservation

Library of Congress Cataloging-in-Publication Data

Names: Burckhardt, Titus, author. | Michon, Jean-Louis, editor. | Fitzgerald, Joseph A., 1977- editor. | Casewit, Jane, 1952- translator.
Title: A living Islamic city : Fez and its preservation / Titus Burckhardt ; with photographs and drawings by the author ; edited by Jean-Louis Michon & Joseph A. Fitzgerald ; translated by Jane Casewit.
Other titles: Library of perennial philosophy. Sacred art in tradition.
Description: Bloomington : World Wisdom, 2020. | Series: Library of Perennial Philosophy. Sacred art in tradition | Includes bibliographical references and index. | Summary: "The Moroccan city of Fez, founded in the ninth century CE, is one of the most precious urban jewels of Islamic civilization. For more than 40 years Titus Burckhardt worked to document and preserve the artistic and architectural heritage of Fez in particular and Morocco in general. These newly translated lectures, delivered while Burckhardt was living and working in Fez, explore how the historic city can be preserved without turning it from a living organism into a dead museum-city, and how it can be adapted and updated using the values that gave birth to the city and its way of life. Aided by photographs and sketches made during the course of his lifetime, Burckhardt conveys what it means to be a living Islamic city"-- Provided by publisher.
Identifiers: LCCN 2020004462 (print) | LCCN 2020004463 (ebook) | ISBN 9781936597666 (paperback) | ISBN 9781936597673 (epub)
Subjects: LCSH: Islamic architecture--Morocco--Fès. | Historic preservation--Morocco--Fès. | Fès (Morocco)--Buildings, structures, etc.--Conservation and restoration.
Classification: LCC NA1590.2.F47 B87 2020 (print) | LCC NA1590.2.F47 (ebook) | DDC 720.88297096434--dc23
LC record available at https://lccn.loc.gov/2020004462
LC ebook record available at https://lccn.loc.gov/2020004463

Cover image:
The Mausoleum-Mosque of Mūlay Idrīs II, Fez, Morocco.
Photograph by Titus Burckhardt.

Printed on acid-free paper in China.

For information address World Wisdom, Inc.
P.O. Box 2682, Bloomington, Indiana 47402-2682
www.worldwisdom.com

Contents

المغرب الأقصى

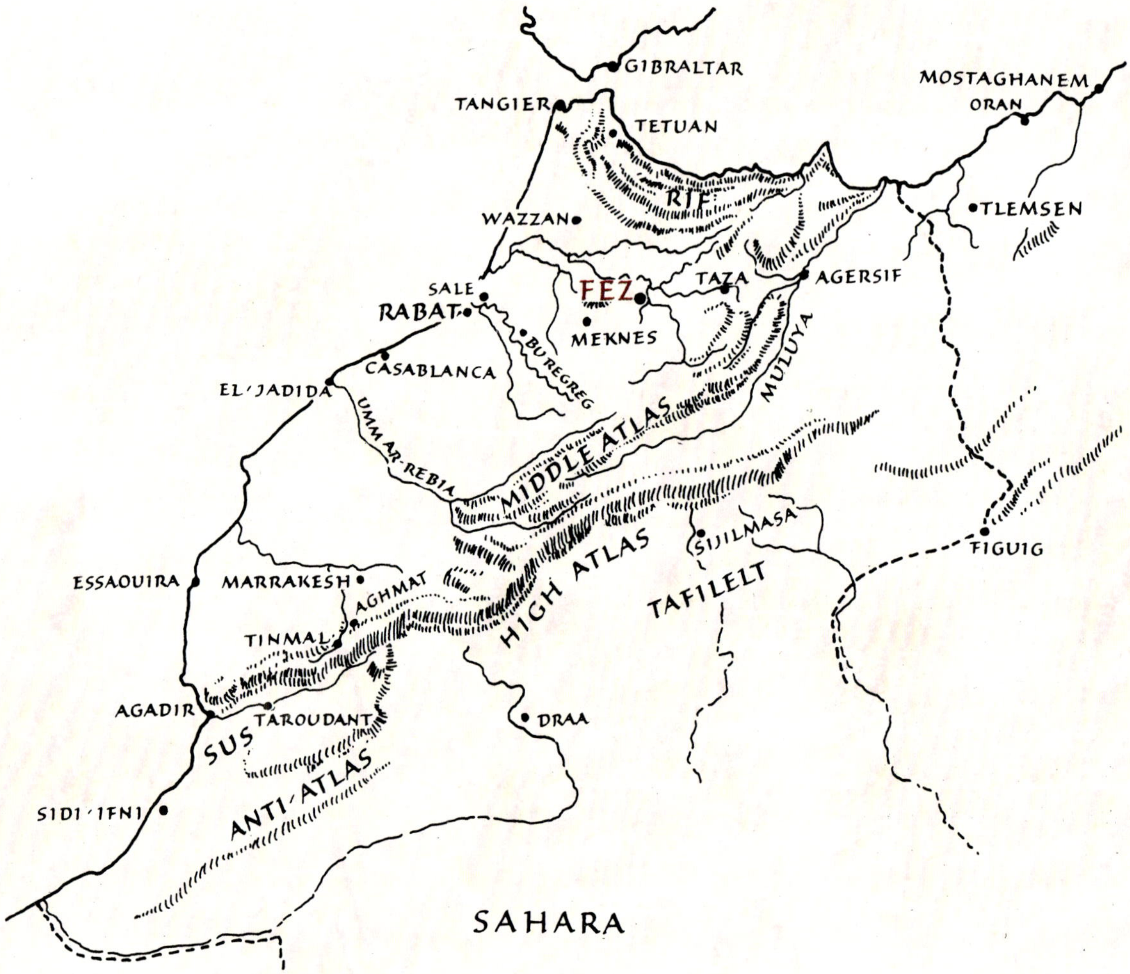

Map of Morocco

Foreword

Between the years 1972 and 1978 Titus Burckhardt devoted himself, through his position with UNESCO, to preserving the artistic and architectural heritage of Fez, one of the most precious urban jewels of the Islamic civilization. During that time he worked on several semi-administrative projects—inventories, proposals, and the like—and, more importantly in this context, delivered numerous lectures to government officials and the general public intended to explain and gain support for his and his colleagues' endeavors.

The reader, however, will soon find that even when Burckhardt talks about a particular technical aspect of town-planning or artistic production, he will invariably show how it is connected in its governing principle to the very nature of Islam. In the author's outlook, one shared by the traditional authorities he intimately knew, Islam is truly all-embracing: for "God is one—there is no god but He"—(Koran 2:163) and "whithersoever ye turn, there is God's Countenance" (2:115).

We are grateful to Titus Burckhardt's colleague and friend, the late Jean-Louis Michon, who made this anthology possible by gathering and thereby preserving these lectures,[1] the majority of which have previously been published neither in French nor in English.[2] Originally separated by time and place, as well as by audience, it is not surprising that the lectures frequently repeat each other in their general themes and even their specific wording.

The current volume takes fourteen of these partially overlapping lectures and refashions them into four distinctive chapters, each with a more or less exclusive focus. This approach seemed to us the most appropriate, despite the modification of the author's text it required,[3] given that writings that were designed *a priori* to be read apart will now be appearing side-by-side.

Nearly all of the photographs and sketches reproduced herein are the author's own and date from the period both shortly before and after the Second World War. As windows into the city's past—and not only the city itself but the way of life that organically formed a part of it—these materials constitute a historical resource whose value will only increase with time. Their present inclusion, in most cases for the first time in an English language publication, provides a further raison d'être for this work.

Finally, a word of thanks is due to the translator, Jane Casewit, for ably rendering the underlying French text into English. In this she was aided by her experience of a quarter century

[1] Jean-Louis Michon acknowledged the assistance of the author's widow, Edith Burckhardt, in performing this task. For more on Michon, himself an authority on Islam and an active supporter of Moroccan traditional life, see the Biographical Notes, pp. 79-80.

[2] See the list of Sources, p. 69, for additional details.

[3] Editorial changes include: the elimination of repetitive passages; the re-arrangement of remaining passages; the re-transcription of foreign words; and the addition of intertextual notes. In order to enhance readability, we have not noted these modifications within the text.

living and working in Morocco, including in Fez itself, as well by the memory of her personal encounters with Titus Burckhardt. She writes, in remembrance, that:

> when he walked through the Fez medina, one felt the presence of a man who not only attracted the respect of passers-by, but who also radiated great sanctity and humility. Venerable old men would greet him warmly, children would kiss his hand, shopkeepers would salute him, and even the ubiquitous cassette vendors would turn off their music when he approached, as they instinctively understood his love of silence and sense of the sacred.

From the foregoing we see that the love the author bore for the city and its inhabitants was requited by the same, and in the pages that follow we will come to learn the deep causes behind his years of service and nearly lifelong devotion.

Joseph A. Fitzgerald

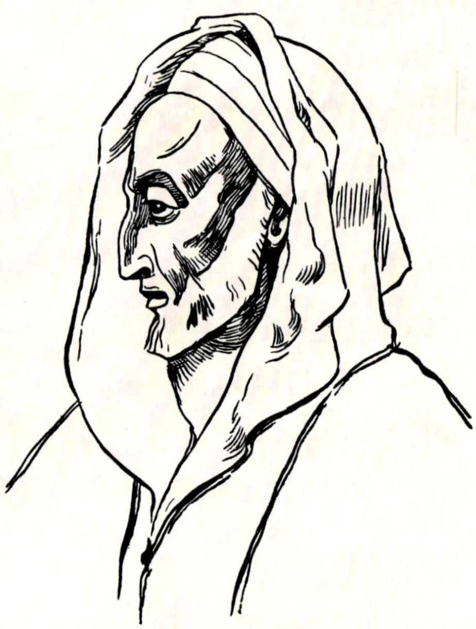

Sketch of a Moroccan elder

Introduction

Titus Burckhardt was born in 1908 in Florence, the son of the well-known sculptor from Basle, Carl Burckhardt. Following upon his early education in Basle he studied art in Munich and in Paris before returning to Basle in order to study art history and oriental languages at its university.

Between 1932 and 1935 he spent extended periods in Morocco where he devoted himself to photography and to the practice of various trades, including that of a shepherd in the Middle Atlas countryside. In Fez he audited classes taught by professors at the venerable Qarawiyīn University, made personal contacts with local craftsmen, and in general became so well known and respected by the inhabitants of the medina, whose clothing and customs he shared, that agents in service of the French Protectorate, offended by his popularity, had him escorted to the Algerian border with instructions never to return to Morocco again.

Based on his lived experience of both rural and urban life and of Moroccan culture, he created a remarkable written portrait, one illustrated by his own photographs and drawings, which in their evocative power are comparable to the sketches of a Eugene Delacroix. This narrative was brought out by Urs Graf Verlag in 1941, under the title *Land am Rande der Zeit* ("Land on the Edge of Time"), but unfortunately it remains unpublished other than in German.

From 1942 to 1968 he occupied a position as director of the art-house press Urs Graf Verlag, where he personally participated in the facsimile reproduction of many of the most ancient illuminated manuscripts of Europe, including the Book of Kells, the Lindisfarne Gospels, the Apocalypse of Gerona, etc. After the independence of Morocco in 1956, he renewed his contacts with the country and the friends whom he had never forgotten. Over the course of periodic visits, he completed his photographic documentation with color slides that enabled him, among other things, to illustrate his book *Fez, Stadt des Islam*[1] which appeared in 1960 in the *Stätten des Geistes* ("Homesteads of the Spirit") series that Urs Graf Verlag had launched upon his initiative.

After retiring in 1968, he continued a fruitful literary career which had already produced the Arabic to French translation of two classic Sufi treaties: *De l'Homme universel* by 'Abd al-Karīm al-Jīlī[2] and *La Sagesse des Prophetes* by Ibn al-'Arabī,[3] as well as several original works on art history, including an illuminating analysis of the principles and methods of sacred art, or *Principes et méthodes de l'art sacré*[4] as this work is titled in French. The year 1972 saw the

[1] Published in English as *Fez: City of Islam* (Cambridge, UK: Islamic Texts Society, 1992).

[2] Lyon: Paul Derain, 1953; second edition Paris: Dervy-Livres, 1976, reprinted 1986. Published in English as *Universal Man* (Roxburgh, Scotland: Beshara Publications, 1995).

[3] Paris: Albin Michel, 1955, reprinted 1974, 1989, 1995, 2008; published in English as *The Wisdom of the Prophets* (Aldsworth, England: Beshara Publications, 1995).

[4] Lyon: Paul Derain, 1958, 1997. Published in English as *Sacred Art in East & West: Its Principles and Methods* (Pates Manor, Bedfont: Perennial Books, 1967; Louisville, KY: Fons Vitae, 2001).

publication in German of a guide to Morocco—*Marokko, Westlicher Orient*,[5] literally "Morocco: Western Orient"—a title by which the author conveys the idea, as he will again in the enclosed lectures, that despite its geographical position at the extreme West of the Islamic world, Morocco is the bearer of a significant patrimony which it received from the Islamic Near and Middle East. It is interesting to note that the appearance of this guide took place in the very year, 1972, when Burckhardt received an offer from UNESCO to participate in a project to conserve the cultural patrimony of the country he had first encountered forty years before and to which he was about to dedicate more than five years of generous and perspicacious activity.

In the spring of 1946, having finished my university studies in Paris, I returned to Switzerland in order to meet with several people, among them Titus Burckhardt, whose articles had appeared in the journal *Études Traditionnelles*. The literary director of this publication, which declared itself to be "exclusively dedicated to metaphysical and esoteric doctrines of East and West," was the philosopher René Guénon, who had become the intellectual guide of a generation eager for ideas and spiritual values. Titus Burckhardt granted me a lengthy interview and indicated that we would no doubt see each other again in the future, as indeed we did; yet as warm as our first meeting was, I could scarcely have imagined that twenty-five years later we would embark upon an extended period of joint participation in projects on Moroccan soil to preserve that country's cultural patrimony.

After three years spent in Damascus as a teacher of English and a student of Arabic, I again returned to Switzerland in order to apprentice as a building designer in an architectural firm specializing in the restoration of historic monuments. Having married, financial reasons forced me once more to change my professional direction: in 1956 I began work as a translator for the United Nations family, and my wife and I thus settled in Geneva, Switzerland. We often went to Lausanne in order to meet with various "friends of Tradition," including Titus Burckhardt and his wife. Each time we re-discovered the warmth of his friendship, the humor with which he recounted anecdotes of daily life, and the wisdom of his answers to the most diverse questions. As for the amplitude of his wisdom and the acuity of his intelligence, these qualities were revealed to me primarily during several meetings we had while I was preparing a doctoral thesis at the Sorbonne on the life and teachings of the Moroccan Sufi Aḥmad Ibn 'Ajība, whose written work and spiritual radiance Titus Burckhardt had encountered during his sojourns in Morocco.

It was in Morocco in the 1960s, during the course of the field and library research I conducted there in order to write this thesis, that I made the acquaintance of Professor Muhammad el-Fassi, Rector of the University of Rabat, who later became State Minister of Cultural Affairs. He honored me with his friendship and it was with him that the idea of an international effort to protect Morocco's cultural patrimony was raised and slowly brought to fruition. In 1968, a pre-project assistance program was submitted to the UNESCO administration. Four years later, after having obtained the consent of UNDP (United Nations Development Program) to finance the project, UNESCO advised the two consultants whose names had been

[5] Olten: Walter-Verlag, 1972.

recommended by the Moroccan National Commission for UNESCO that they were the chosen experts charged with assessing the status of the country's cultural patrimony, the dangers that threatened its integrity, and the measures required to ensure its preservation.

Titus Burckhardt, then aged sixty-four, had never before had professional dealings with international organizations and it was my privilege and pleasure to participate with him in his first encounter with the United Nations system. Before being allowed to leave on our assignments, we were both obliged to undergo a several day's long briefing on administrative procedures that took place in a residence in the outskirts of Paris, where we spent hours listening to the recorded accounts of other experts recently returned from assignments. Despite being meant to facilitate our adaptation to local conditions, we could not but chuckle at many of these accounts, as, for example, when one such expert solemnly forewarned us that before leaving for Morocco we must prepare ourselves for anything, absolutely anything, to happen!

Titus Burckhardt obviously had no need of such warnings, for he knew the country exceedingly well and so, like a doctor running to his patient's bedside, he left his peaceful place of retirement above Lake Geneva to come and relieve the invalid's pains—pains whose origins he had long ago identified and whose progress he had followed. Several days after the end of the training program we made our way to Morocco separately and met in Rabat for our first meetings with officials from the Ministry of Culture.

According to the provisions of their engagement contracts, each expert was in charge of a particularly fragile sector: for Titus Burckhardt, it was that of historic sites and monuments, and for myself it was that of the traditional crafts. This distribution of labor, while reflecting the separation between different UNESCO departments, in no way corresponded to the reality of the field, since the conservation of traditional art and that of historic monuments depend closely upon each other. If the restoration of monuments relies on the contribution of craftsmen who have mastered traditional techniques, no less do experienced craftsmen, in order to live with dignity, rely on connections with regular programs of architectural conservation.

Given these considerations, and with the agreement of the heads of the relevant divisions in the Ministry of Culture, we established a unique action plan involving work in three main areas of activity: traditional crafts, historic sites and monuments, and cultural affairs. The division of tasks between the experts was made on a geographical basis, the only one that seemed rational and capable of responding to the indicated needs without any duplication or overlap of work. Titus Burckhardt settled in Fez to attend to issues related to the deteriorating urban fiber of the medina, while I stayed at my post in Rabat to liaise with the central administration and to travel to wherever important assets of patrimonial heritage were seen as being endangered. Throughout the duration of our assignment, we met with each other frequently to exchange observations and coordinate their activities.

Burckhardt's work in Fez fell into two distinct phases lasting two-and-a-half years each. During the first phase, he dedicated himself to two fundamental tasks: cultural affairs and the inventory of the medina's sanctuaries and great houses. In the second phase, Burckhardt became the cultural advisor to an international group of specialists assigned to develop an urban masterplan for greater Fez.

Lecturer and Inventory Taker

Burckhardt was well aware that no project to preserve architectural patrimony would have any chance of implementation unless those responsible for doing so, together with a majority of the population concerned, were fully convinced of the usefulness of such an undertaking. He therefore began to give lectures, in Fez and other cities, whose purpose it was to expound and promote the value of the artistic treasures and the living human resources, particularly in the domain of craftsmanship, of which Morocco was the depository, as well as to underscore the need to utilize and conserve this exceptional patrimony.

The subject of the lectures (chapters 1 and 2) collected in the first section is the city of Fez, inasmuch as it formed the framework for a way of life which, for over a millennium, was shaped by the Muslim population in response to its needs. We learn that Fez was founded by a king and his son—the two Idrīses—under the banner of piety and religious knowledge and that, since its origin, Fez has always grown according to criteria which attempt to guarantee the integral development of every citizen's personality, that is to say, his physical integrity as well as psychological happiness and spiritual aspiration. There exists, therefore, a typically Islamic form of town-planning based on the idea that man is the representative—the caliph—of God on earth and that the entire city should be a place conducive to the remembrance of divine Unity (*tawḥīd*).

The principal theme of the following lectures (chapters 3 and 4) is that of art as a means of expressing the beauty of creation, and thus of the Creator. One comes to understand the "why" of the craftsmen's choice of forms when building and decorating mosques, religious schools, and civic buildings, including houses and palaces with their inner courtyards which isolate them from the outside world. In each case, the craftsman respectfully continues the ancestral traditions which have embellished the city and bestowed upon it the status of protective sanctuary (*ḥaram*); hence the need to adopt measures to ensure the maintenance of the high-level craftsmanship required for any program of architectural rehabilitation to succeed.

In the same period Burckhardt began to compile an inventory of the medina's sanctuaries (Appendix I) and another of its great homes, an action more than justified by the fact that a great number of these buildings had never been catalogued in view of their classification and conservation, even though many are of significant architectural and historical value.

Cultural Advisor

The second phase of Burckhardt's assignment in the medina involved his participation as a cultural advisor on a multi-disciplinary team of national and international consultants forming the Fez Master Plan Workshop.

To describe Burckhardt's role within this organization and the influence he had upon its members, we can do no better than to refer to part of the account of Stefano Bianca—one of the Workshop's principal associates who worked alongside Burckhardt for three years on the project to preserve the old city of Fez—presented on the occasion of a Homage to Titus Burckhardt in 1999 in Marrakesh.[6] Let us then listen to the vivid testimony of this architect and town-

[6] Stefano Bianca, who now directs the Aga Khan historic cities program in Geneva, was unable to attend the celebration of this "Homage," but copies of his contribution were distributed to the participants. It was published in French as "Quelques souvenirs personnels de ma collaboration avec Titus Burckhardt" in *Sagesse et Splendeur des Arts*

planner, still young at the time, who has managed to find the right descriptive words allowing us to share the company of a man of exceptional quality whom he considered as his "master."

> In 1972, UNESCO had assigned him as a consultant to inventory the architectural patrimony of Fez and to evaluate its present state of conservation. Realizing that a simple annotated catalogue of the monuments would be insufficient, he pleaded in favor of establishing a master-plan for greater Fez, one offering a complete and realistic framework for the rehabilitation of the old city. It was on his recommendation that I was able to join the interdisciplinary team of UNESCO consultants to whom this task was entrusted from 1975 to 1978.
>
> Titus Burckhardt's dedication of nearly six years of his life to the cause of Fez was in response to a debt of gratitude he felt to a country and a city which, during the decades of the thirties and forties, had so amply nourished his spiritual development. Beyond that, it seems to me that his immense devotion arose also from the challenge posed by his vision that Fez—the best preserved example of a still-living historical Islamic city—could serve as a model of continuity, showing a traditional urban form's ability to evolve while maintaining its intrinsic qualities. Although a committed conservationist, he was realistic enough to admit the necessity of taking modern needs into account if one wishes to preserve and maintain the viability of the old city. On the other hand, he was the first to oppose a certain type of modernization which is content to import and impose models and procedures without evaluating their impact and without adapting their physical structure to social habits and local conditions. His thinking in this respect, often expressed with a striking lucidity and poignant realism, offered a precious lesson to the team of professional architects and town-planners.
>
> The UNESCO team was installed in a colonial-era courthouse, the old *maḥkamah* of Bāb al-Hadīd, a pseudo-traditional building with numerous small cells grouped around two courtyards which were surrounded by arcades and galleries. Titus Burckhardt occupied one of these compartments. He often said that it was a great improvement compared to the tiny "monkey cage" that the Minister of Culture had first wanted to give him at the entrance of the Batha Museum. During all these years, and despite the privileges he could easily have enjoyed, Burckhardt was the most conscientious and reliable of the team members, always available wherever his presence was required. Later I came to learn that alongside the heavy professional burden he shouldered, he

---

islamiques—Hommage à Titus Burckhardt (Marrakesh: Les éditions Al Quobba Zarqua, 2000), pp. 13-20; and in English as "Titus Burckhardt (1908-1984): A Personal Reflection" in *Sophia: The Journal of Traditional Studies*, Vol. 5, No. 2, 1999, pp. 185-192.

It should be noted that the above-cited French book includes several other articles—in particular those of Philippe Faure, Mahmud Erol Killiç, Jean-Pierre Laurant, Jean-Louis Michon, Kamil Khan Mumtaz, James Morris, Muhammad Suheyl Omar, and Seyyed Hossein Nasr—a fact which speaks to the influence that Burckhardt, through his literary work and broad personality, exerted across the globe.

still found the energy in his free time to work on preparations for the World of Islam Festival which took place in 1976 in London, and of which he was the instigator and a guiding spiritual force. It was for this event that he also had published his major book: *Art of Islam: Language and Meaning*.[7]

Over the course of the years we worked together in Fez, I had the opportunity to become better acquainted with Titus Burckhardt and to observe several facets of his human relationships. It was enjoyable, and sometimes amusing, to see how his personality commanded the respect even of those who had little in common with him or whose opinions radically diverged from his own. His introspective nature did not prevent him from being a skillful negotiator nor even, when necessary, from manifesting shrewdness in defense of a good cause. He entered only rarely into polemics, but by a single pithy remark, drawn from an area overlooked by his peers, he would reduce their arguments to nothing or else expose the poorness of their hypotheses. Sometimes, the team was surprised to see his ideas suddenly sketched on a piece of paper, for few knew that this son of a sculptor was also an accomplished artist, with innate creativity. This gift, combined with his knowledge of esoteric traditions, was at the origin of the unique approach by which he perceived craftsmanship as lying at the base of Islamic art.

His treatment of the Moroccan authorities was always polite and refined, almost ceremonious, despite his later disappointment with the inefficiency of the central administration, crippled as it was by bureaucracy and internal rivalries. It was a special pleasure to observe the relations he maintained with the medina's inhabitants. Simple people were instinctively attracted by his radiant authority and would sometimes through touching gestures show the respect and veneration they felt for him. Often, when accompanying him in the old town, I had the spontaneous sense that he was walking about disguised as a Westerner.

In the last year of his stay in Fez, Titus Burckhardt and I, together with Hassan Fathy, Jean-Louis Michon, and others, were engaged as planning advisors for a new university campus in Mecca (1978-1981). The Saudi authorities, fond of American efficacy, had chosen for their project the Chicago-based design firm of Skidmore, Owings, and Merrill (SOM), and had then appointed a committee of advisors charged with supervising the formulation of the plan and instilling it with the basic principles of Islamic architecture. It was no easy task for us to make a group of this sort function, and the efforts as well as the good will of the SOM architects were sorely tested since several of them abandoned the task in the course of the exercise.

It took some time for the American team to understand that we were neither simply looking for attractively drawn models coated with Islamic ornaments, nor for copies of historical monuments, but were in search of something

[7] London: World of Islam Festival Publishing Company, 1976; second edition: Bloomington, IN: World Wisdom, 2009.

> which, in its scale, rhythm, urban texture, and correct interrelation of spaces, buildings, and rooms, would embody the spirit of Islamic architecture. The meetings were stormy at times, with Hassan Fathy suddenly rising up like a master of arms among his musketeers. A more meditative Burckhardt would hold back until, solicited by others, he would speak out at last. Then he would bring together all the arguments in an extraordinary manner and, viewed under this different light, the questions naturally found their answers.

After reading the lectures, notes, and projects gathered in this collection, many will have understood that the philosophy and key-ideas which animated Burckhardt—even though they were warmly welcomed by large audiences and shared by his fellow colleagues to the point that the 1978 Urban Master Plan bears throughout its entire structure the mark of Burckhardt's ideas—are perspectives that have found few echoes of support over the course of the past decades. Nevertheless, if one considers the two sectors to which Burckhardt attached the most importance in the cultural realm, namely traditional art and architectural patrimony, it is undeniable that these can afford considerable advantages, both material and spiritual, for the collectivity which agrees to ensure their management.

Burckhardt encouraged the venerable city to revive a partially ruined patrimony by presenting, among other things, a project for the restoration and promotion of historical monuments in the center of the medina, as well as a project to establish a center for the study of Arabic and Islamic sciences. Offering university level courses, the center would be open to students of all countries and all faiths, with instruction to be delivered by Moroccan scholars using traditional pedagogical methods. A bridge would thus be built among cultures, one which would be efficacious if, according to the terms Burckhardt employed, "its fruit is the respect for every authentic spiritual patrimony."

It may yet be that some institution or individual will become aware of these projects and take an interest in implementing them. Were this to happen, the publication of this collection would not have been in vain—but "it is God who is the guarantor of success," *wa'Llāhu waliyyut-tawfīq*.

Jean-Louis Michon

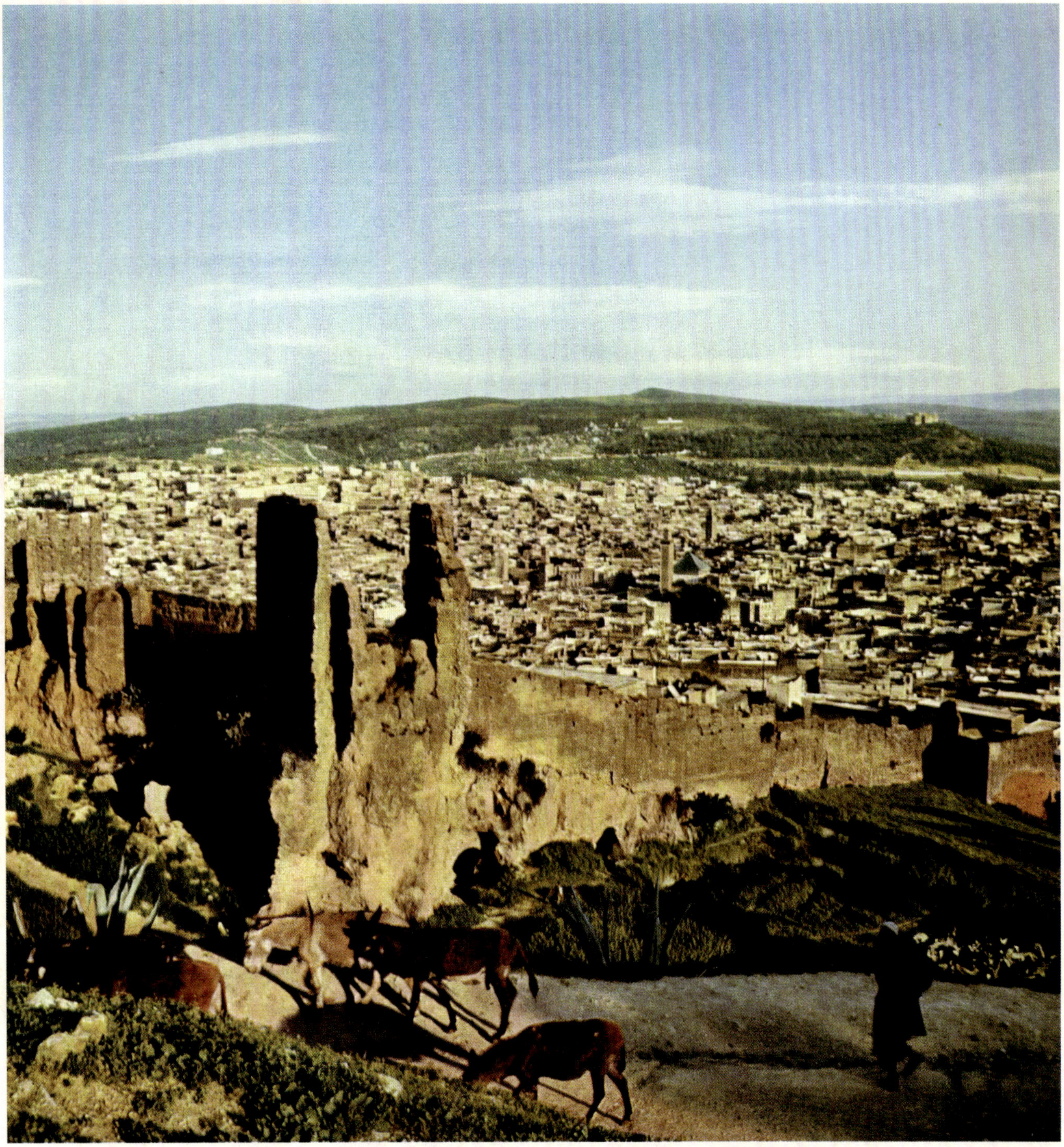

View of the middle of the old city of Fez, seen from the north. Note the green pyramidal roof and minaret of the Mūlay Idrīs II Mausoleum-Mosque.

Author's Preface

The old city of Fez, the city of Mūlay Idrīs,[1] is still here in all its dignity and beauty, an incomparable monument to a great civilization and deep faith; but we know that its existence is threatened by both inner and outer factors. If the Moroccan government makes no effort to save it, our descendants will no longer have the joy of contemplating this astonishing agglomeration of ocher crystals, dominated by some hundred minarets. Fez is not only the history of Morocco, it is also the history of the Arabo-Andalusian world and ultimately of all of Muslim civilization.

I often hear it said that a developing country like Morocco has more than enough to worry about besides preserving an old city like Fez, which in any event is doomed from the start by those of her own sons who leave her to live elsewhere. Instead of spending money to keep some old walls standing, would it not be better to build hospitals, factories, and schools, or even a cultural center where the youth could come into contact with expressions of modern art?

As natural as it may be, the question is poorly formed. First of all, the preservation of historic monuments can perfectly well coincide with the populace's economic interests, as is proven by the direction tourism has taken. Secondly, and above all, there is no common measure between the promotion of necessarily temporary social progress, which must be continually renewed, and the preservation of a cultural treasure, which, once lost, can never be recovered.

During the French Revolution, many abbeys and cathedrals were destroyed, among them some of the most beautiful works of medieval Christianity, such as the great monastery of Cluny. Others were simply abandoned to the destructive forces of nature. What is the use, one asks, of spending state funds in order to preserve the witnesses of a bygone era? Today, one may ask in return, how many cities with no more than a few remnants of such buildings would not pay double, even a hundred times, what these buildings cost their builders so long ago, were it possible to rebuild them?

How can such a situation be explained? Are we, or are we not, capable of replacing works that have disappeared with others, just as valuable? It is necessary to respond in the negative: there is something in every perfect work belonging to the past which cannot be repeated. Mankind may bring about all manner of progress, in the current sense of the word, but it will never again find on this path the disposition of soul and spirit that allowed it to create such works as the Hagia Sophia, the Mosque of Córdoba, the Cathedral of Chartres, or the Qarawiyīn Mosque. There is something unique and inimitable in these masterpieces of art, particularly in those created not by isolated individuals but by a whole collectivity, those which are the expression of a whole culture and a deep faith. The city of Fez is a work of this kind, not only on account of the great monuments it contains but also, and above all, owing to its totality, which represents an exceptional example of Islamic town-planning.

Let us consider the enormous financial and technical effort involved in an archeological rescue operation such as the one needed to preserve for us the Egyptian temples of Abu Simbel, or the one currently being undertaken to prevent the Buddhist temple of Borobudur from

[1] See p. 4.—Editors' Note

sinking. The cost of each of these operations is much higher than the original cost of the artistic execution of the works in question. What feeling, then, drove those who financed and organized the rescue work of the monuments we have just mentioned? They were aware of the fact that certain perfect creations of the human spirit cannot be repeated, and are never replaced; and yet, these works belong to man, to all of mankind—they are like aspects of our soul. They are ours to the extent that we grasp their beauty and perfection. Were they to disappear, something of our own soul would vanish; something of ourselves would be forgotten.

Thus it is with the old town of Fez: it is a collective work, perfect in its own way, of a certain human world, a world rooted in faith and molded by an *adab*, a culture of the soul and spirit. It can be replaced by something else, but can never be substituted by a work of the same quality.

One might suggest that the appreciation of old works is the prerogative of a certain historically oriented culture which implies distance in relation to the objects that it studies and admires. It will be said that Moroccans have just emerged from the Middle Ages and need first to absorb the advantages of the modern world, before leaning to the past; at the cultural stage where they find themselves, the preservation of historic monuments is a luxury. This reasoning, which we have heard from the mouths of Moroccans, leaves out one thing: the acquisition of new means of knowing and acting should not come at the price of the loss of our identity. Now, the guarantee of this identity is precisely cultural patrimony. This includes many components, among them language and the forms of thought that language conveys; it also certainly includes visual art, especially its expression in architecture, and everything else that makes up our daily environment. What our ancestors put into the forms of their environment, this acts anew upon us, their heirs; there is nothing that exercises a greater influence on a man's soul than the environment which surrounds him. Or rather, yes, there is something that comes before, and that is dress, for nothing influences our attitude as much as dress. Architecture comes next: firstly, the architecture of interiors, then architecture in general, and finally, the architecture of a city, town-planning. As a result of this, the need for art is not a purely aesthetic question; art is a vital reality which man could never do without.

It is not necessary, or should not be so, to teach a Moroccan child the history of Islamic art in order for him to grasp the beauty and truth of traditional Maghribi art. The values of this art are derived totally from the principles of Islam, from the Arab and Berber genius, and from the Moroccan soil. As long as these realities remain, there is no reason to relegate past works of Maghribi art to the status of museum objects, reserved for specialists.

There is presently much discussion of the cultural needs of the youth, who are impatient to learn about everything that makes up the modern world, that is modern science and modern art, the latter including techniques of painting, theater, music, and so on. To promote culture, we are told, would be to satisfy these needs. But this is to forget about proper education, the goal of which should never be the satisfaction of desires but the awakening of a critical sense capable of distinguishing between the good and bad, the beautiful and ugly. Now, this critical sense, should it not be exercised *a priori* through the support of and in the field of cultural patrimony itself? In other words: should one not, above all, open the eyes of young Moroccans to the beauty of their country's own traditional art? The preservation of artistic monuments is, therefore, the work of education, and this work is all the more worthwhile because, unlike certain sciences, it addresses not just the brain but the senses, heart, and spirit as well.

I have often had the occasion to take European friends, cultivated and sensitive people, through the old city of Fez. I used to fear that walking up and down the twisting streets would quickly tire them, that the muck of a rainy day would disgust them, and that the overpopulation—the dense throng in the marketplaces—would discourage them. But nothing of this was able to lessen their enchantment which was summed up in words like these: "Finally, a human city!"

I meditated on these words. It is certainly true that next to an ever more mechanized world, leveled down and dehumanized, the old town of Fez represents an environment where life unfolds according to an eminently human rhythm. But there is something more. This life, of which Fez is like the crystallization, calls on all of man, who, as indicated above, has physical needs, an affective life of the soul, and an intelligence which goes beyond both planes. Considering these things, there exists no order or custom in old Fez which does not possess this integral character. And this is no surprise since everything flows from the *sunnah*, the Prophetic tradition, for which man is still at once body, soul, and spirit. One cannot, therefore, neglect any one of these modalities without harming the entire human being.

Titus Burckhardt

Inscription in Kūfic style of the "Blessing on Muhammad," commonly found in Moroccan mosques and schools

I

A Model City

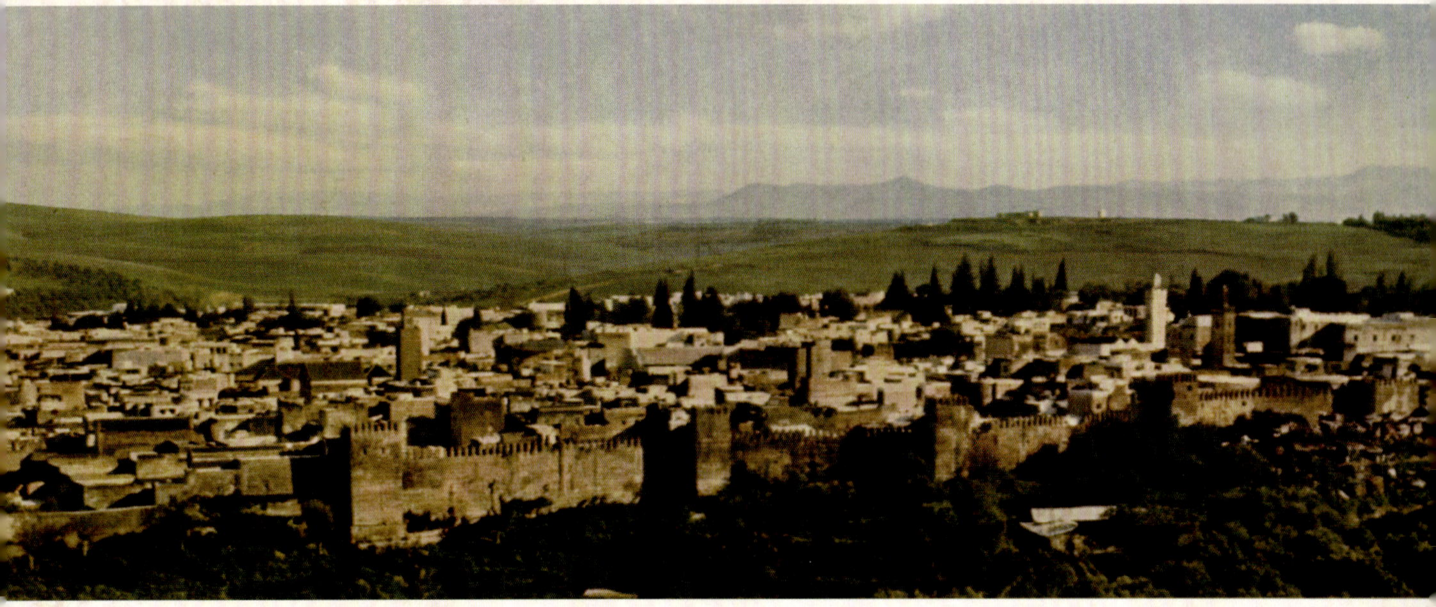

Above: View of the upper part of the old city of Fez, seen from the north;
Below: Plan of Old Fez and New Fez (Fās al-Bāli and Fās al-Jādīd)

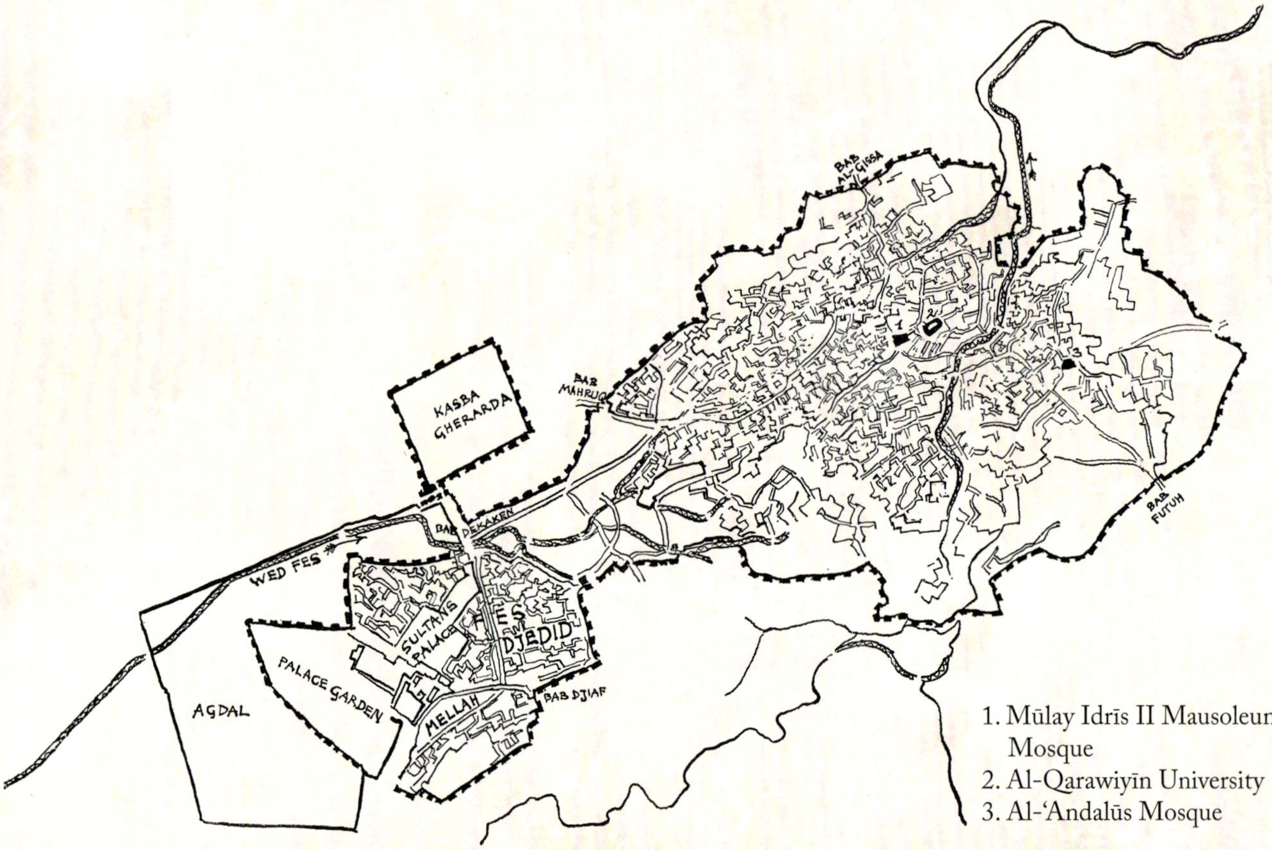

1. Mūlay Idrīs II Mausoleum-Mosque
2. Al-Qarawiyīn University
3. Al-'Andalūs Mosque

Chapter 1

Constants of Arabo-Islamic Urbanism

Among cities which, through their architectural form and spiritual vocation, remain irreplaceable witnesses to great civilizations, Fez represents a particularly complete and homogeneous example of the Arabo-Islamic city. Its exemplary value, however, consists not only in the considerable number of historical monuments housed within its walls—including some, such as the famous university mosque of al-Qarawiyīn, which date back to the third century of the Hijrah (ninth century AD)—but above all because it represents a perfectly coherent urban whole, of homogeneous style, in harmony with the site, and integrating life's various aspects—housing, commerce, craftsmanship, education, and worship—into an equilibrium that is at once logical and spontaneous.

It is precisely this synthesis that we can define as town-planning or as *urbanism*, using the expression here in all its fullness, since the *urbs*, the city, concerns the whole of man. It is difficult to say to what extent this "urbanism" results from a conscious and consistent planning or from a type of collective intuition. We know, in any case, that certain elements of general importance such as the fortifications, bridges, water system, university colleges (*madāris*), and the great mosques, are the work of kings. Other public service works, of no less importance, were provided by the pious foundations (*awqāf* or *aḥbās*):[1] the Koranic schools, baths, and the caravanserais (*fanādiq*). Finally, there are urban projects started by a king and continued by groups of citizens, such as the water system discussed below.

All these initiatives, be they individual or collective, guarantee Unity and are framed within that tradition which, in an Islamic country, can only be an ever-renewed application of the *sunnah*, the Prophetic custom. It must be understood that this tradition is not grafted *a posteriori*, as a sort of idealistic direction, onto the concrete data of life; on the contrary, the *sunnah* provides above all the models for practical life. By regulating daily activities such as the way of eating, for example, or of washing, the *sunnah* determines the form of living. Moreover, by determining the most humble, the most "down-to-earth" things, the *sunnah* shapes men's souls and, at the same time, the "style" of communal life. The *sunnah* is "realistic" in the sense that it always envisages the integral nature of man, who is at once body, soul, and spirit—bodily gestures having their repercussion in the soul and spiritual convictions being reflected in outward behavior. This global vision of the human being inspires traditional town-planning, and it is this that essentially distinguishes it from modern town-planning, which tends to dissociate these different domains of human life.[2]

[1] This institution plays a large role in every Muslim city. In Fez, the real properties which are *ḥubs* or "mortmain" items are estimated at more than one third of the buildings of the old town. In other words, they are made "immovable" at the wish of their donors, to the profit of public works of all kinds.

[2] In addition, it is not surprising that we often have to endure aesthetic atrocities in modern cities: a harmony of forms can only be realized in a spiritual universe.

We mentioned the water system as an example of collective town-planning. This involves the artificial division of the water of the Wādī al-Fās over the entire stretch of the old city, an eminently important work for a Muslim city wherein water is at once the guarantor of fertility, a factor in hygiene, and the element of ritual purification. In all likelihood, the site of the city, founded in 192 Hijrah (808 AD) by Mūlay Idrīs II, was chosen in view of this use of the river. This site is a valley between two plains at different levels; the water from the upper plain, which has many springs, has to flow across the valley. From a strategic point of view, the position of the city is far from ideal since it can be dominated from the surrounding heights, but the abundance of water makes up for this. Since the valley is curved, like a shell or amphitheater, it is possible to distribute this water over practically the entire extent of the valley.

The Wādī al-Fās is captured on the upper plain, to the west of the city, and flows towards the highest point of the valley's bank where it remains in an accumulation basin before being divided into several branches which spread out over the entire eastern-facing side of the valley; these branches are then further divided into multiple canals whose waters feed the public and private fountains and fertilize the gardens, before being gathered by the sewage system which carries the city's waste into the Wādī Abū al-Kharārīb, a watercourse which runs along the bottom of the valley and joins the great Sibū River on the plain below. The same water system is repeated on the other side of the valley, where the Wādī al-Zaytūn, rather than flowing directly into the Wādī Abū al-Kharārīb, is made to flow across the valley's western-sloping bank so as to supply and purify that part of the town. The Wādī al-Zaytūn is connected to the Wādī al-Fās by a canal that descends from the accumulation basin and allows the flow of the two rivers to be regulated.

Let us point out that participation in the water system is inseparable from private property: to buy a house is to inherit the right to share in the river's water. This institution, which is both communal and private, goes back to the city's founder, Mūlay Idrīs, who purchased the water of the river in perpetuity from the neighboring tribes as a gift to the town's inhabitants. We believe that this order of things—this coincidence of private rights and urban rights—is an important characteristic of Muslim towns in general.

The only visible elements of the entire canalization network of the Wādī al-Fās are the reservoir basins—located at the highest point of the old town, in the Abū al-Jalūd gardens—together with several principal canals originating from them. One of these canals is directed towards the Sharābliyīn quarter at the north of town, where its waters trace a long arc before reaching the Wādī al-Zhūr; another goes down towards the town center, and a third crosses the garden district at the city's southern end. Distributors in the form of turrets are located at various "knots" on the system and measure the exact amount of water coming to each private house. The greater part of this network is underground and is known only to the masters of the *qwādsiyah* profession, the "canal workers" or "sewage workers." The water that feeds the fountains they call "sweet" or "fresh" (*al-mā' al-ḥālu*), and the water that takes away the waste they call "bitter" (*al-mā' al-marr*). They say that the water of such-and-such a conduit is "dead" when it has been used for domestic purposes.

This system has been very aptly compared to the circulation of blood with its separate arteries and veins. The enclosed gardens and orchards within the city's ramparts are irrigated thanks to it; the patios of countless homes are

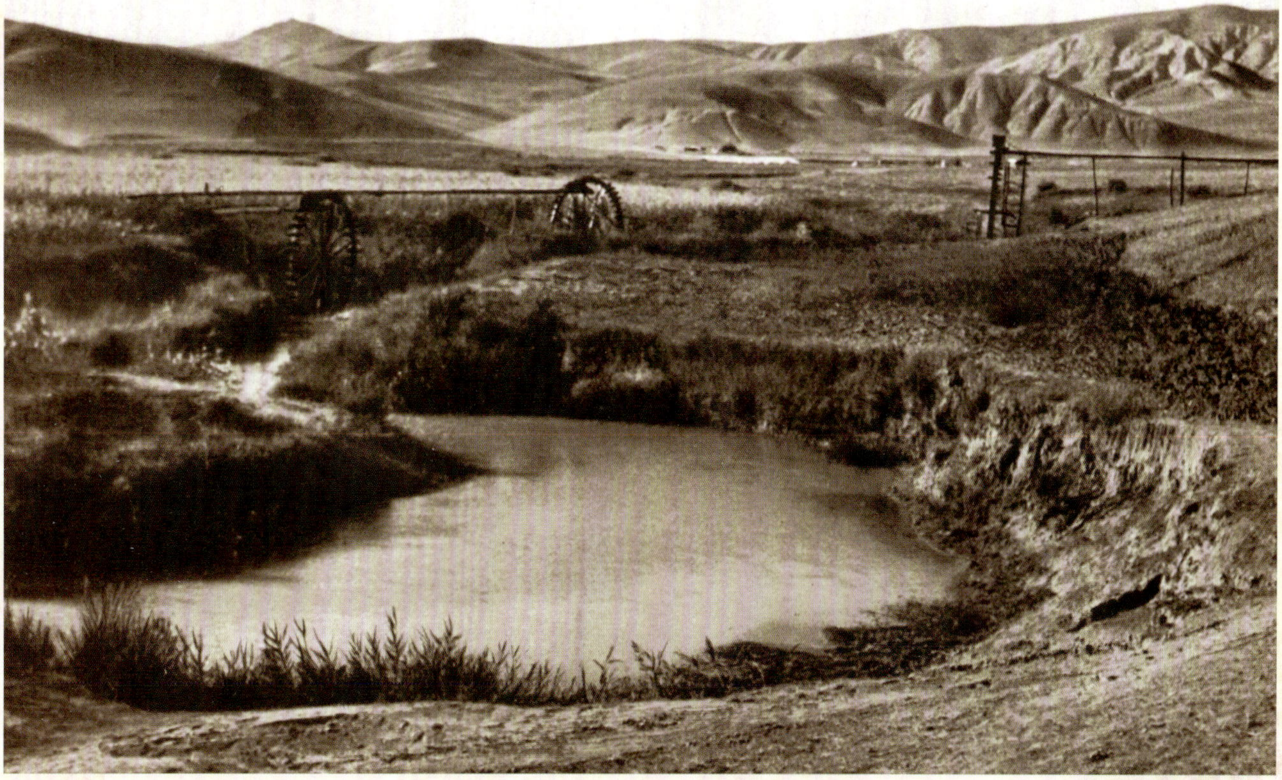

Above: View of the Sibū River on the plain below Fez. Notice the water-driven bucket wheels irrigating a corn field; *Below left*: Close up of a bucket wheel; *Below right*: A young farmer (*fallāḥ*) harvesting steppe grass.

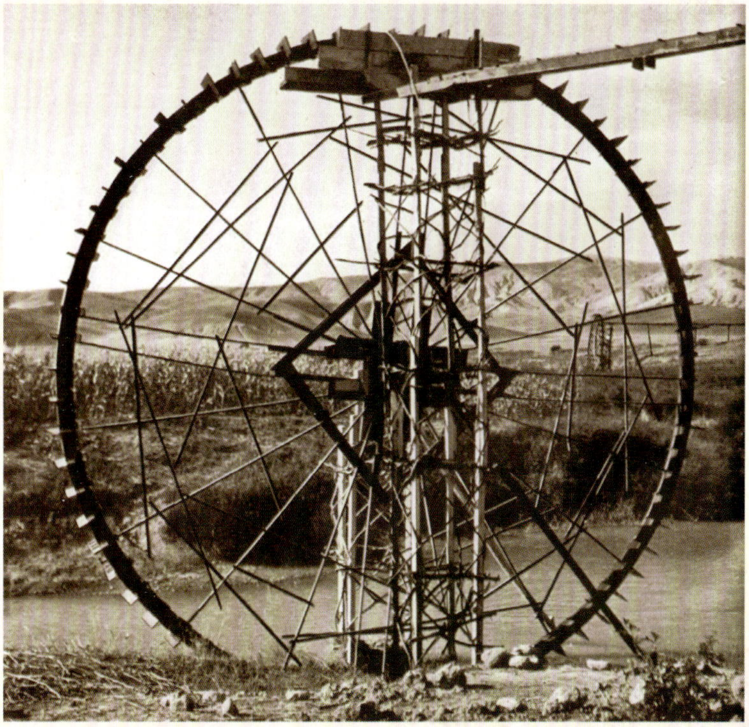

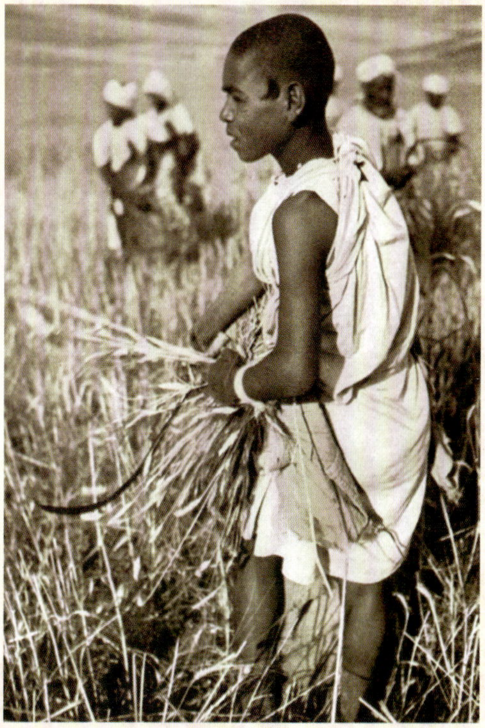

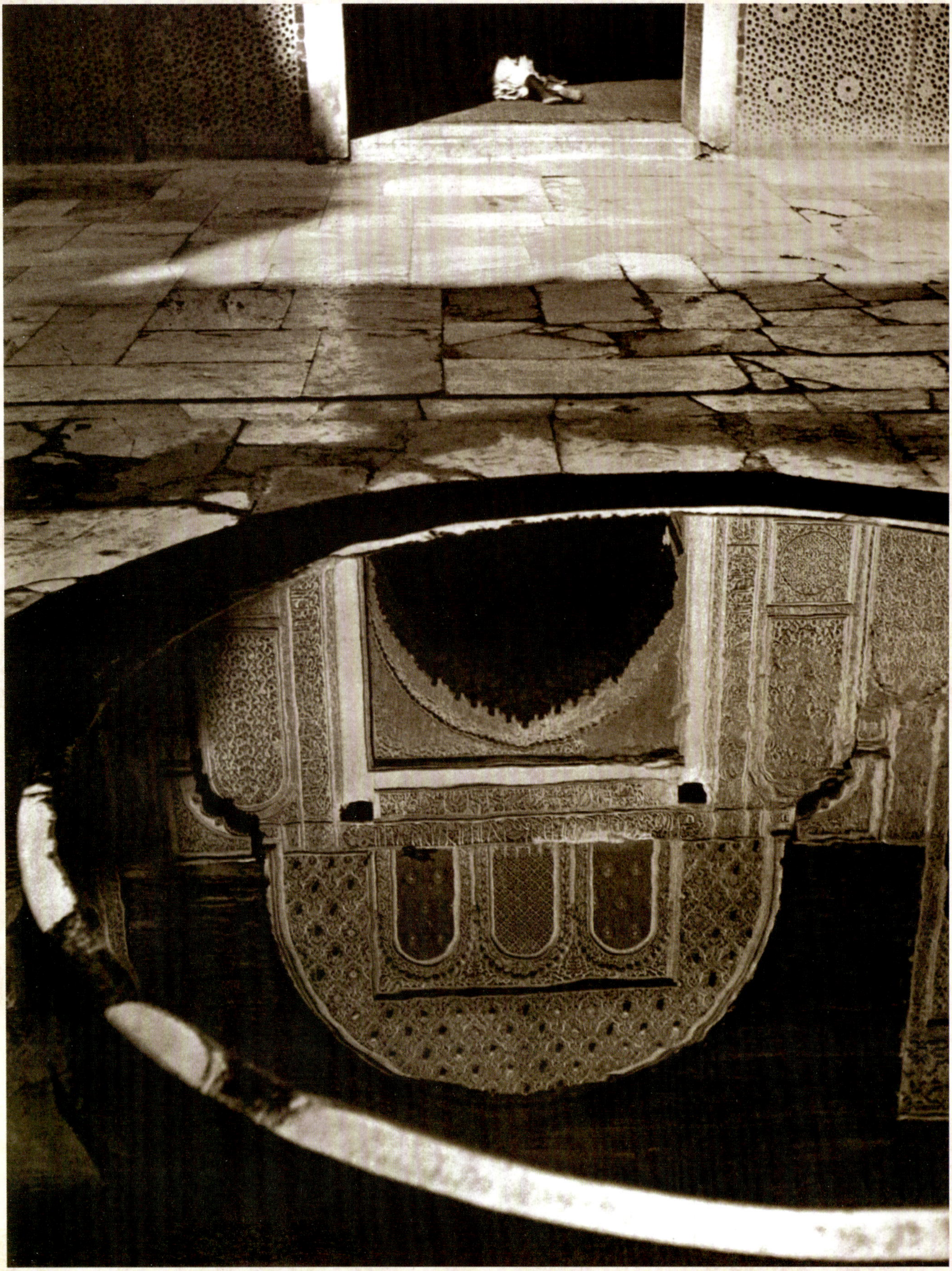

likewise brought to life by the singing of water, and the mosques' fountains never run dry. Water is the foundation of all life: "From water We made every living thing," says the Koran (21:30). It delights the soul—its dancing spray on the basin is the very image of joy—and, on the spiritual plane, it is the symbol of purity of the heart. Water is necessary for the body, soul, and spirit alike, and nothing could better illustrate the principle of traditional town-planning than this triple use of water.

Today a modern distribution system frequently supplements the old river water system. The *wādī* water is no longer used for drinking, but only for washing, watering gardens, and for ablutions, following the Shariate principle that all flowing water is pure. This is an instance where, in our era of the machine and overpopulation, the vulnerability of traditional institutions appears. It could, in fact, be asked whether the progressive pollution of the water table of the plain traversed by the Wādī al-Fās will not end by destroying the power of regeneration normally inherent to all natural watercourses. It is easy to notice the thin oleaginous film that already covers the accumulation basin of the Abū al-Jalūd garden.

Most medieval cities of Europe and the Near East are laid out according to the design of the Roman cross with its two axes, the *cardo* and the *decumanus*. One would search in vain for some rectilinear plan like this in the layout of Fez, whose streets very simply retrace the routes of the caravans. Starting from three gates—to the west Bāb Abū al-Jalūd (or, more exactly, Bāb al-Maḥrūq), to the north Bāb al-Jīssah, and to the southeast Bāb al-Futūḥ—its main thoroughfares descend towards the town center located on the valley floor. The ramparts of Fez have many other gates and one of these—Bāb al-Hadīd, the "Iron Gate"—bears a name that is a reminder of the old caravan traffic. For several centuries, however, almost all the traffic has gone by the three previously mentioned gates. Transport coming from the south and east—from the region of the Gharb, most notably Tāfīlālt—arrives, or arrived, through Bāb al-Futūḥ, while transport from the north—from the region of the Jabal—went through Bāb al-Jīssah. This arc went through the town center and crossed the river, thus joining the two sides of the city which, in the distant past, made up two distinct urban entities.

The arc we are describing is sometimes simple and sometimes comprised of an array of thoroughfares, each relatively narrow, made uniquely for pedestrians and saddle or pack animals. The use of animal-pulled carts was apparently never taken into consideration, no doubt because the surrounding countryside always remained open to the crossing of nomadic and semi-nomadic tribes who would not have tolerated the existence of passable roads in their territories. Here is another characteristic common to many Arab towns: the contrast between the closed and fortified city, with its essentially sedentary life, and the open countryside with its nomadic life—a contrast, as Ibn Khaldūn well describes, that is full of human potential, the city being renewed through the Bedouin contribution. The contrast, or complementarity, in question, is furthermore reflected in the town itself, where a continual exchange between the urban and outside population takes place. But, to come back to the question of roads, a street was deemed sufficiently wide if two laden mules could pass by one another, though in certain places such as Bāb al-Nuqbah or in the Darb Abū al-Ṭawīl, only one animal at a time went by and this resulted in a whole *adab* of traffic which is still applied today.

The transport of merchandise in town was facilitated by the existence of the *fanādiq*

Opposite: Fountain in the courtyard of the Madrasah al-'Andalūs

(plural of *funduq*) which correspond to the caravanserais and khans of the cities of the East. They are at the same time hotels and merchandise warehouses, and their distribution along the main thoroughfares perfectly marks the stages of commerce: near the gates are the *fanādiq* with stables for the pack animals, nearer the center are the warehouses for the raw craft materials, and right near the central marketplace are the depots for the finished goods. A man coming from the countryside to the city could secure his mount in a *funduq* before proceeding into the central marketplaces, for entering an Arab city is a little like entering a house. Whereas the thoroughfares of a European city generally give out onto open squares, those in an Arab town like Fez lead towards the covered and ever-more intimate alleyways of the souks (*aswāq*; singular *sūq*). There the visitor seeks direct contact either with the merchant or with the maker of certain objects, the craftsman being a seller at the same time. All the life of the souk, with its display of goods and its loud sales cries, is so made as to eliminate superfluous intermediaries and to adjust prices to their lowest level; the economy of the souk fluctuates, and it relies on human contact.

The twisting and turning of the access ways can also have a defensive function analogous to that of an obstacle course. An enemy's army, having overcome the gates of the city, would have had great difficulty in penetrating to the town center, where were to be found both its riches and the seat of its power, that is the souks of precious goods and the Qarawiyīn University, whose members could potentially appoint or remove a sultan. We are alluding here to the power of the *'ulamā'* to "bind and loosen," in the people's name, the pact (*bay'ah*) of fidelity to the king. It was on this power of the college of learned men that the true authority of the city of Fez was founded, as well as its relative autonomy in regards to its kings. Moreover, the fact that the royal city—Fās al-Jādīd, with its palace, its garrison-kasbah, and its banking quarter (its Jewish quarter or mellah)—is located outside the university and commercial city expresses perfectly the relationship between the two authorities.[3]

It might be objected that this whole urban order only functions on its own scale, that of man and animal, and not of the machine. We do not deny this, neither do we necessarily see this as negative; on the contrary, that areas are forbidden to motor vehicles is good. The most visited old city in Europe is Venice, where automobiles cannot circulate—this is a consolation and a promise for Fez.

The core of an Arab and Muslim town is always a marketplace located in the shadow of a sanctuary,[4] the sole exception being in the case of a royal city built around a palace. The central marketplace—together with the entire commercial quarter—is an area not only of commercial exchange but also of manufacturing; raw materials flow to it and leave it again in the form of created objects. The hub of public life is here: the city thinks, hopes, and fears whatever the souk thinks, hopes, and fears. As for the residential quarters, they are located outside the marketplaces and preferably toward the periphery of the city—this in conformity with the *sunnah*, which calls for the separation of public or collective life and private or familial life.

[3] In the fourteenth century the kings of the Marinid dynasty built a royal city further upstream on the Wādī al-Fās, on the edge of the upper plain and at the very place where they could, if necessary, deny water to the inhabitants of the old city. Today, this royal city's ramparts are linked with those of the medina.

[4] The central marketplace is normally reserved for precious objects such as fine textiles and jewels. This *qīsāriyyah* has its own gates which are closed at night.

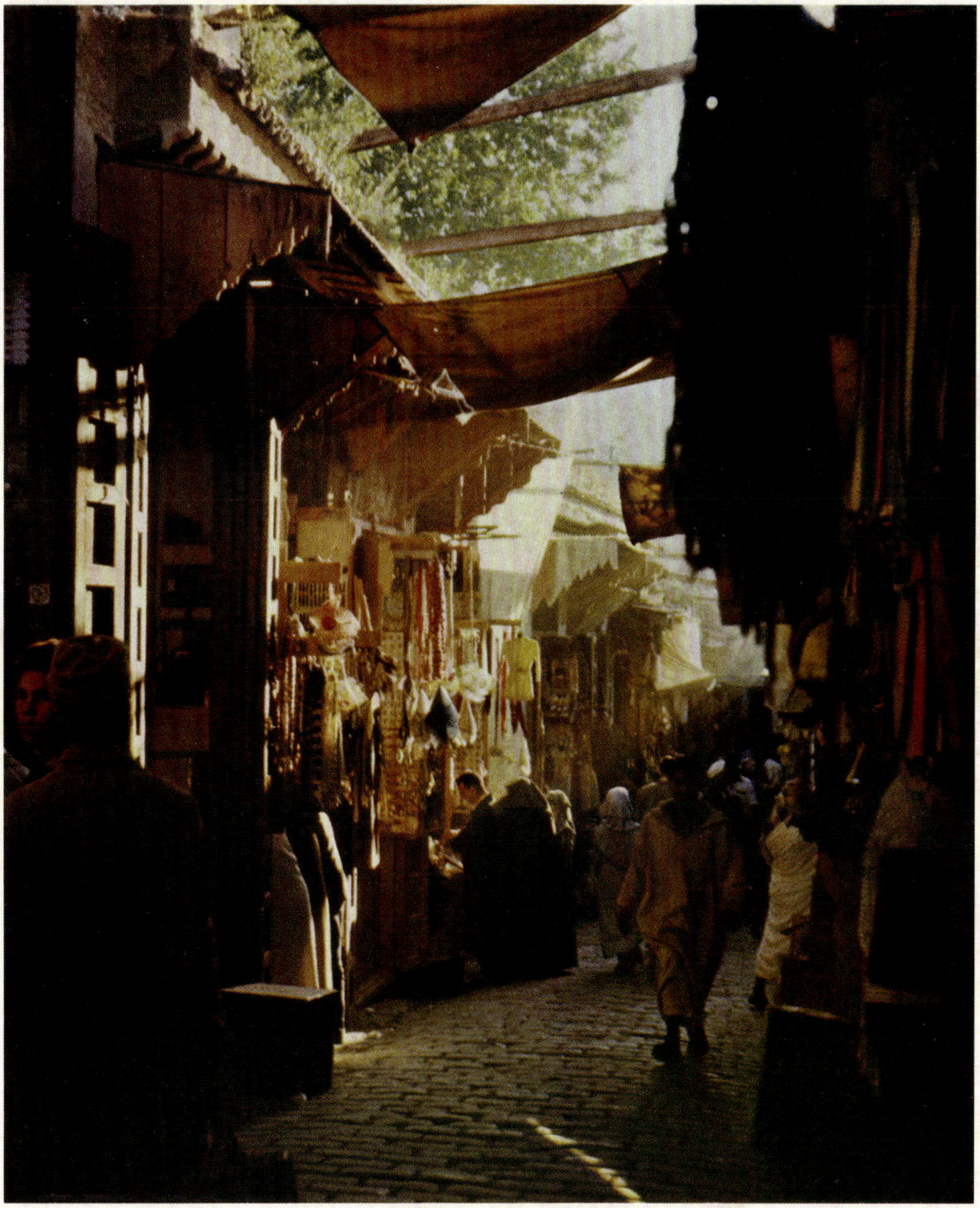

Souk al-'Attārīn, the spice market

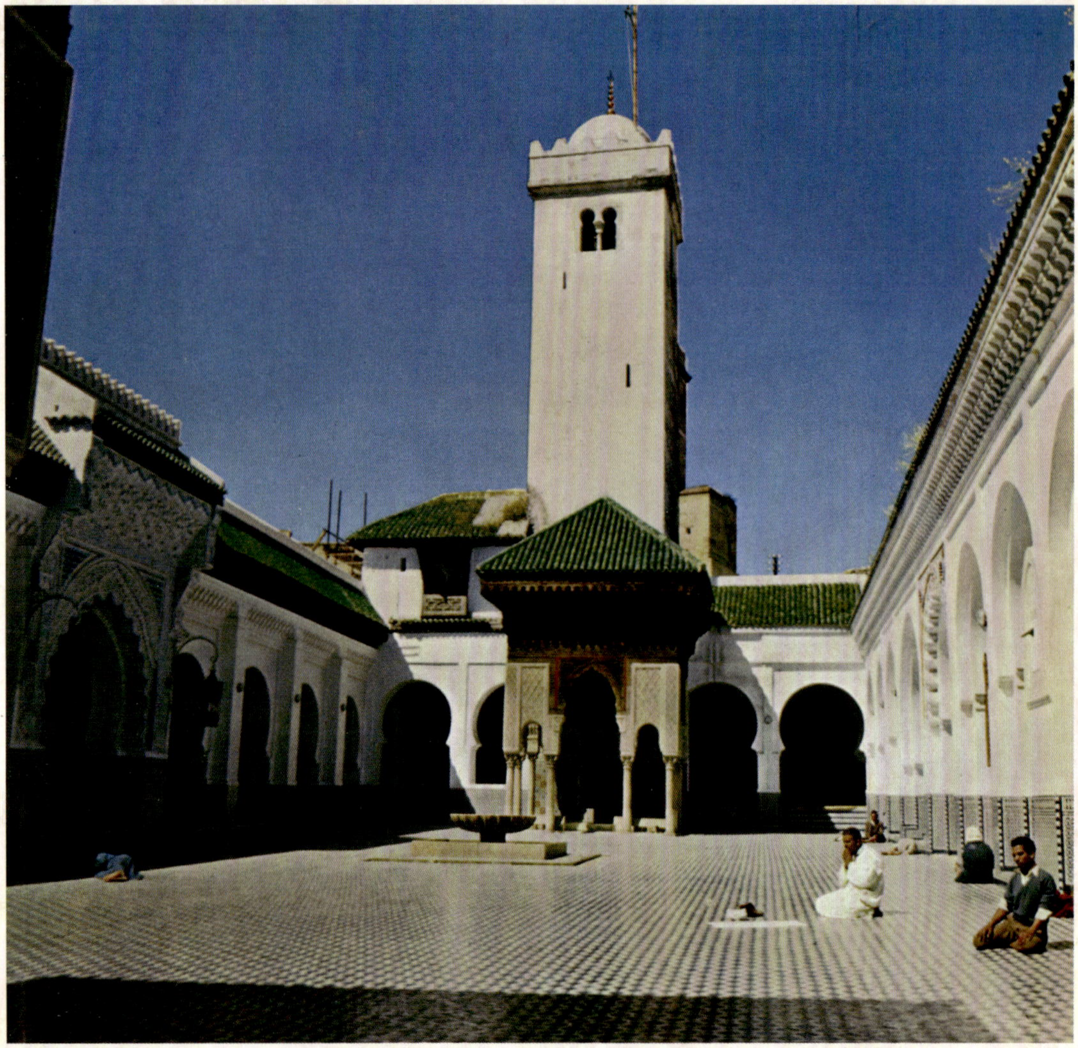

Courtyard of al-Qarawiyīn University-Mosque

In Fez the central marketplace sits between the two largest sanctuaries, which are like the two poles of intellectual and spiritual life: the mausoleum-mosque of the city's founding saint, Idrīs II, and the university-mosque of al-Qarawiyīn. The first—the object both of pilgrims and of criminals seeking asylum—is like the city's heart, whereas the second is its brain. In a certain sense, the Mausoleum-Mosque of Mūlay Idrīs was the center of the religious brotherhoods to which almost all the members of the craft guilds belonged, whereas the university-mosque of al-Qarawiyīn represented the center of intellectual life. The influence of the one and the other on urban life was incalculably great.

One thing to recall: the influence the contemplative or religious brotherhoods exerted in the craft circles proves that manual trades were always considered as a support for spiritual perfection and, in any case, as a way of life compatible with the contemplation of spiritual realities. The same craftsmen were often assiduous auditors at the courses in

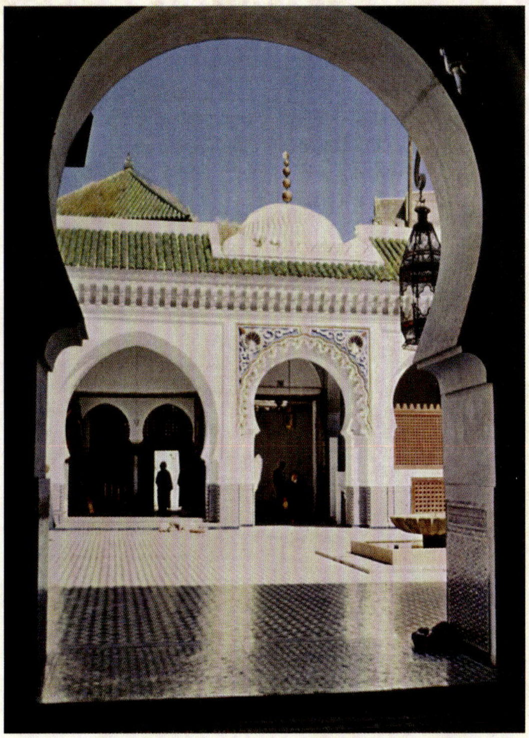

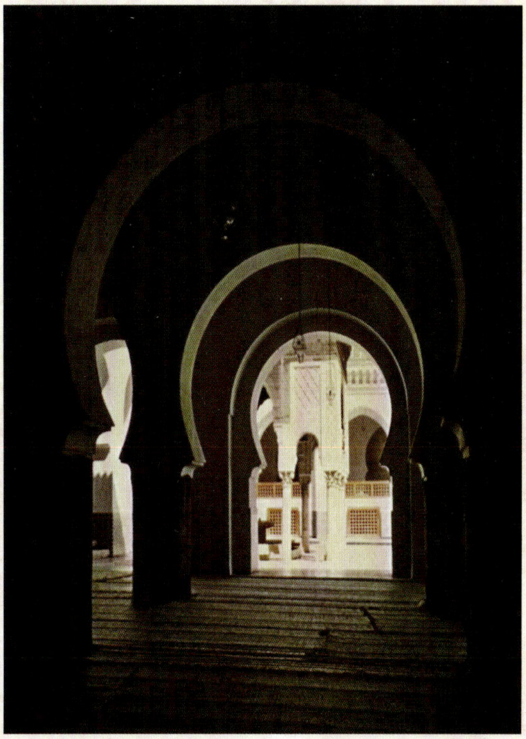

Above left and right: Views of the courtyard and hall of al-Qarawiyīn University-Mosque;
Below right: Outer wall of the Mūlay Idrīs II Mausoleum-Mosque, with beggars seated

Islamic learning given publicly in the Qarawiyīn Mosque. The practice of placing the main marketplace close to a sanctuary and, in a way, beneath its protection goes back to the pre-Islamic example of Mecca as confirmed by the Koran, according to which there is no harm in combining a visit to the sanctuary with the seeking of profit or "a bounty from your Lord" (2:198). According to this point of view, the sanctuary is not the least profaned by its proximity to the marketplace; it is the marketplace that is blessed by the sanctuary.[5]

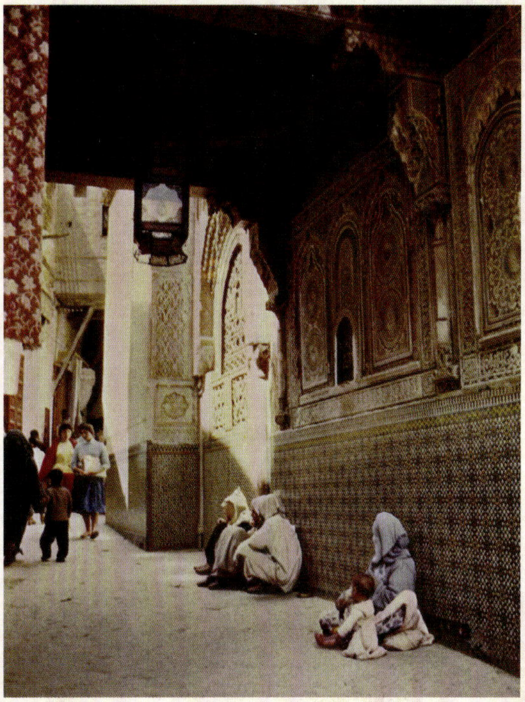

[5] According to another, quite different, perspective, the great mosques with their inner courtyards—that of the Mosque of al-Qarawiyīn is the largest unoccupied space within the medina—correspond to the forums of Latin cities, for it is there that the active population of the town flocks together in the event of a common danger.

Seen from the height of one of the surrounding hills, the city of Fez displays a marvelous homogeneity of forms, reminding one of a geode of crystals; it is only with difficulty that one can discern the contours of single houses. Its fundamental unity is the *bayt*, a long and rectangularly-shaped habitable room, whose average size is fairly constant. Several *buyūt* (plural of *bayt*), grouped around a central courtyard, make up the house, which can always be enlarged by adding new *buyūt* or by juxtaposing several inner courtyards. There is the simple house, whose courtyard is generally surrounded by four *buyūt*, and there is the *riyāḍ*, the enclosed garden that can be made of two *buyūt* connected to each other by perimeter

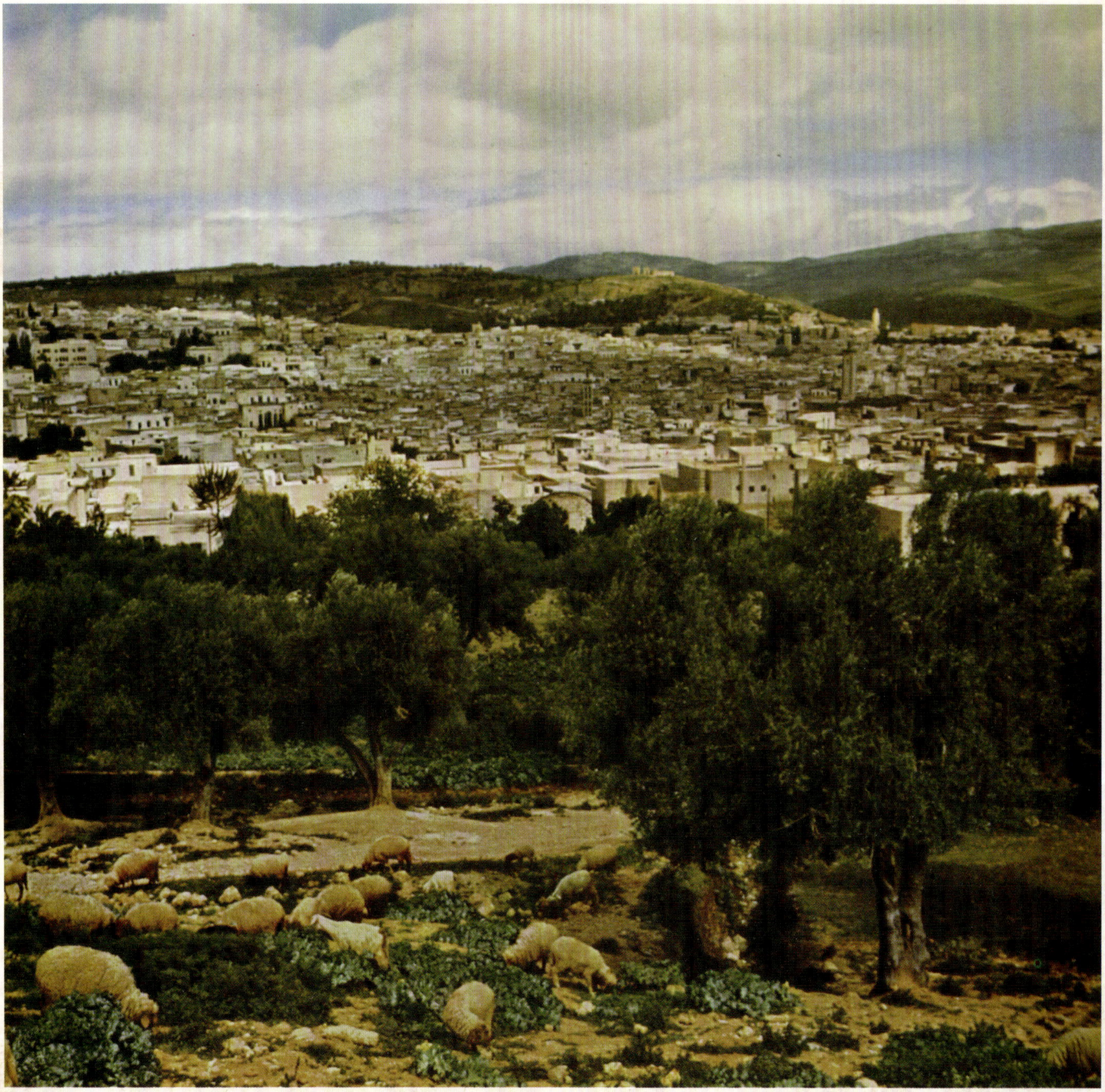

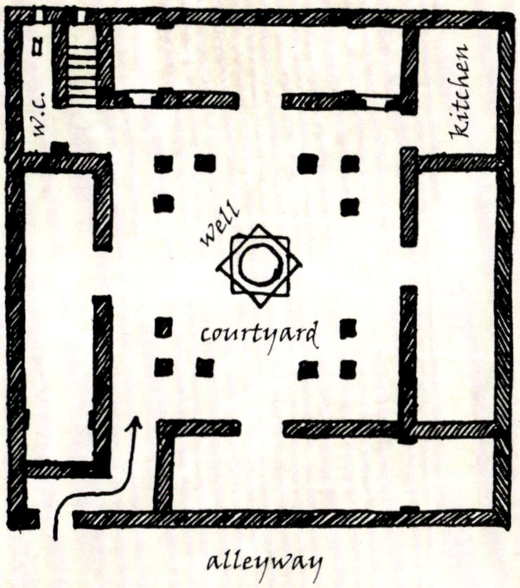

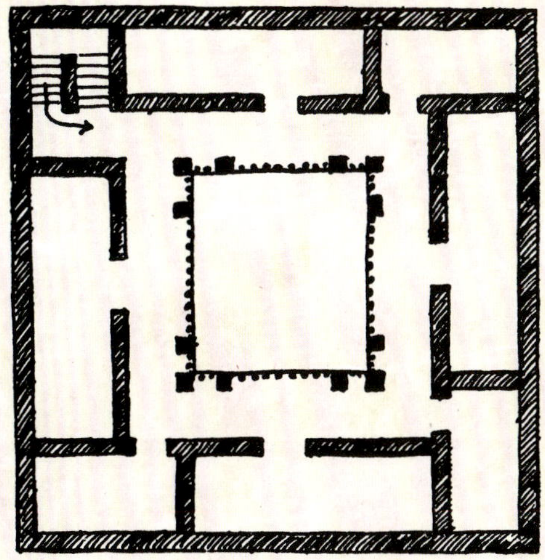

walls. Around a large courtyard, the *buyūt* will be relatively larger but their proportions will remain approximately the same.

Arabo-Islamic architecture always develops starting from a basic habitable unit or *corps de logis*, which is repeated at various scales of size depending upon the circumstances. Even palaces are made up of a more or less complex grouping of units and have often been expanded depending on successive landlords, each one adding several new rooms. With the exception of fortifications, this architecture never proceeds from great masses of structures, and nothing is more foreign to its genius than the European concept of buildings built in blocks and subdivided into multiple apartments. Herein lies the difference between a collectivism determining individual existences based on a preconceived whole, and a "personalism" operating in the framework of an adaptable collectivity.[6]

Above, above left, and below:
Drawing and plan of the ground and upper floors of a typical house in Fez

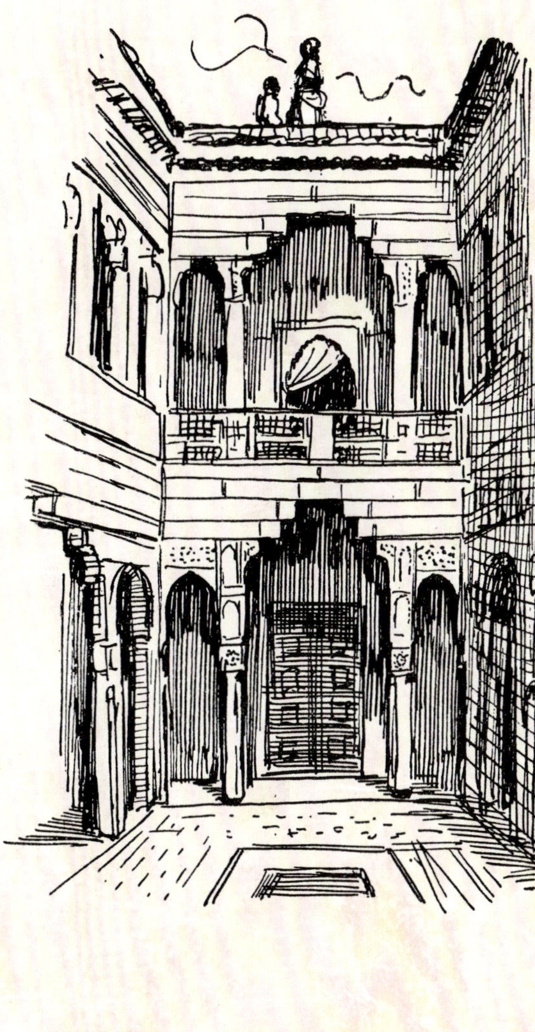

[6] One might object by saying that the two concepts belong to two different eras and that modern life demands forms of modern habitation. But this argument does not excuse the construction of apartment blocks inside a historic city like Fez. It is perfectly possible to adapt new construction to the urban structure we have just explained.

Opposite: View of Fez from the south

Much has been said about the egalitarian character of Muslim society, but it is too often forgotten that its apparent leveling hides the utmost internal differentiation. On the one hand, all men are equal before God, for all are but weak creatures or servants (*'ibād*, plural of *'abd*), and in this sense the individual effaces himself in the collectivity; indeed, just as he effaces himself in the mass of those who pray, in the anonymity of the crafts, and in the uniformity of traditional dress, so too the individuality of each house or dwelling hides itself in the compact mass of city buildings. On the other hand, each man, by the fact that he is a responsible creature before God, is unique in his inner nature, and it is in this transcendent uniqueness that his liberty and dignity reside. In the same way each Muslim dwelling opens onto the sky, in its solitude.

Fez is not a museum-city: it is an intensely living organism, well fitted to the measure of man, but the shock of too abrupt a confrontation with the modern European world has disrupted it greatly. What is imperative now is to preserve the city's irreplaceable monuments and essential characteristics at the same time as realizing a measure of adaptation to present exigencies. Such adaptation necessarily involves modernization but, at the same time, it must be inspired not by European models but by what we might describe as the urbanism inherent in the ancient structure of the city. To attain this end, there will be many obstacles to overcome, not the least of which is the prejudice in certain circles against what is regarded as a "return to the Middle Ages."

Before "modernizing" the old Arab city by "Europeanizing" it at the same time, let us consider the human order its structure expressed. It may well be that this order bears values unknown to modern town-planning, values which are independent of whether rammed earth or concrete is used and which, in their essential motivation, are independent of "eras" since they are enshrined in a spiritual perspective.

And let us not forget that there still exists in Fez what we would call a *genius loci*, or, more adequately, a *barakah* that will have the last word.

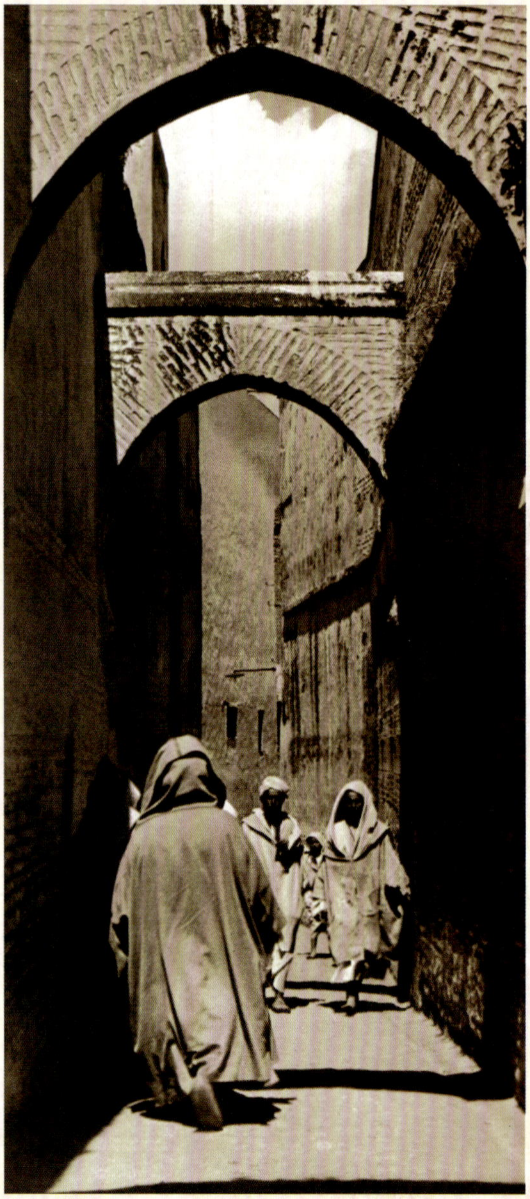

Above and opposite:
Streets in the old city of Fez

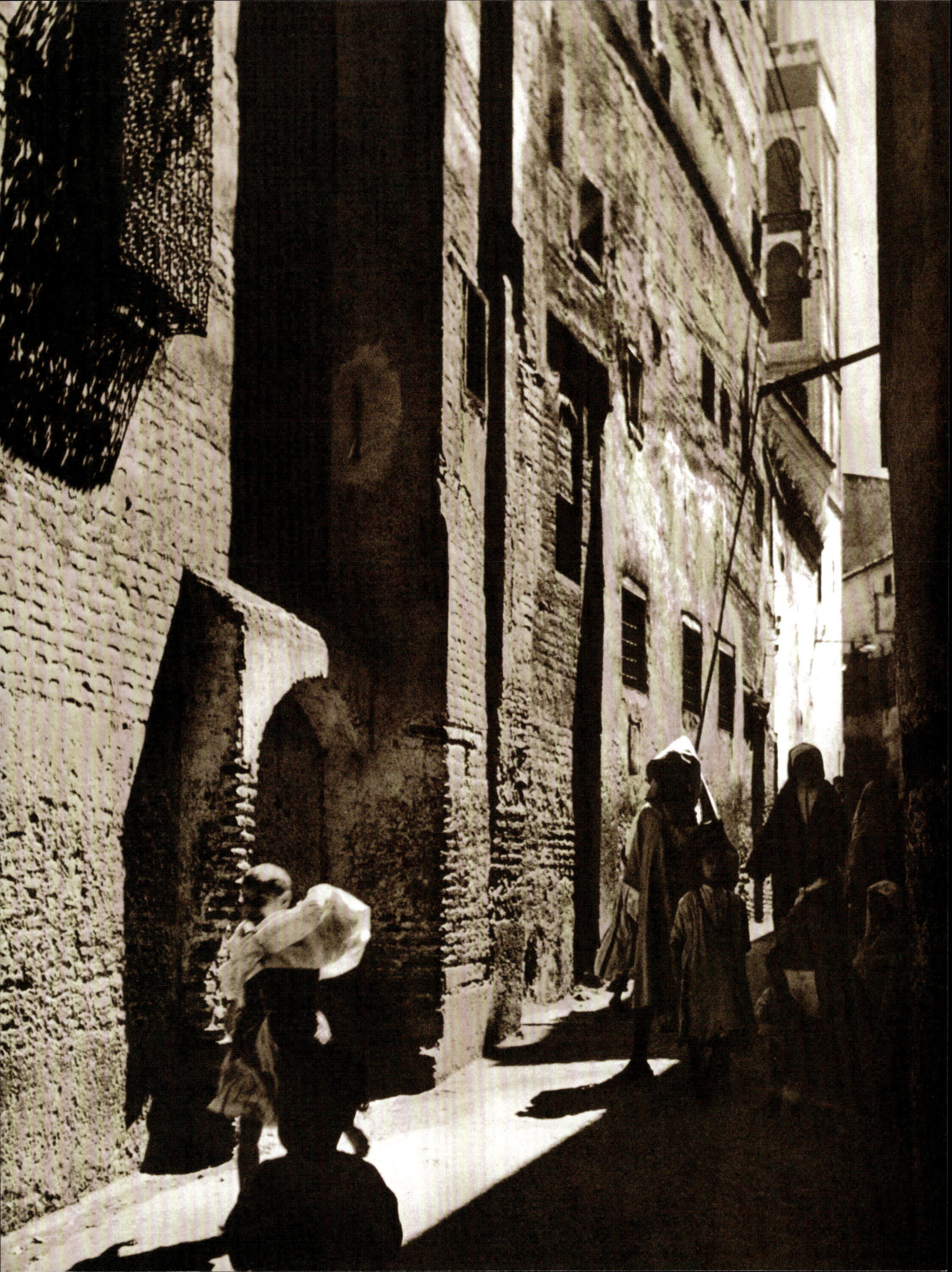

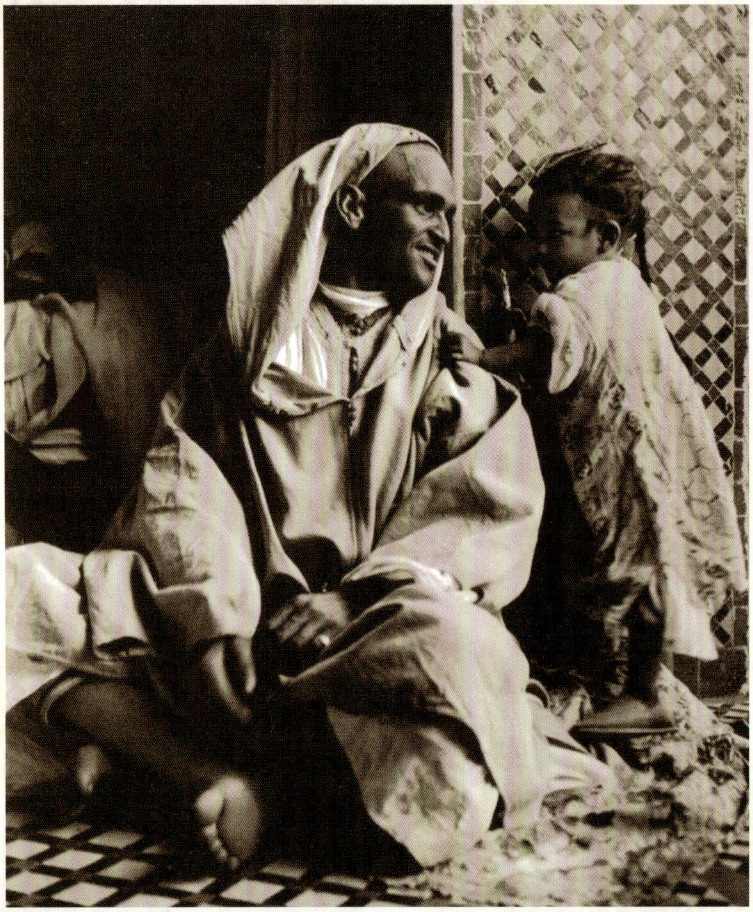
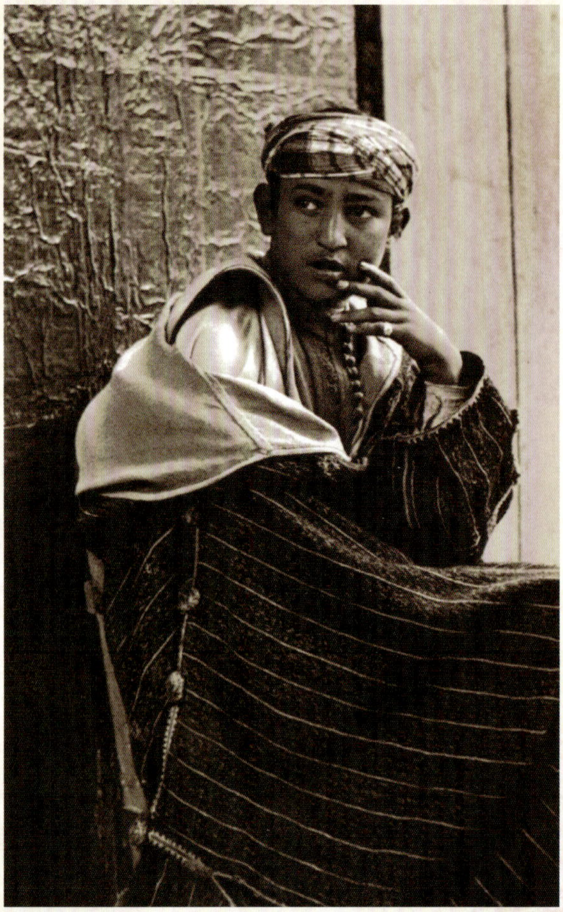
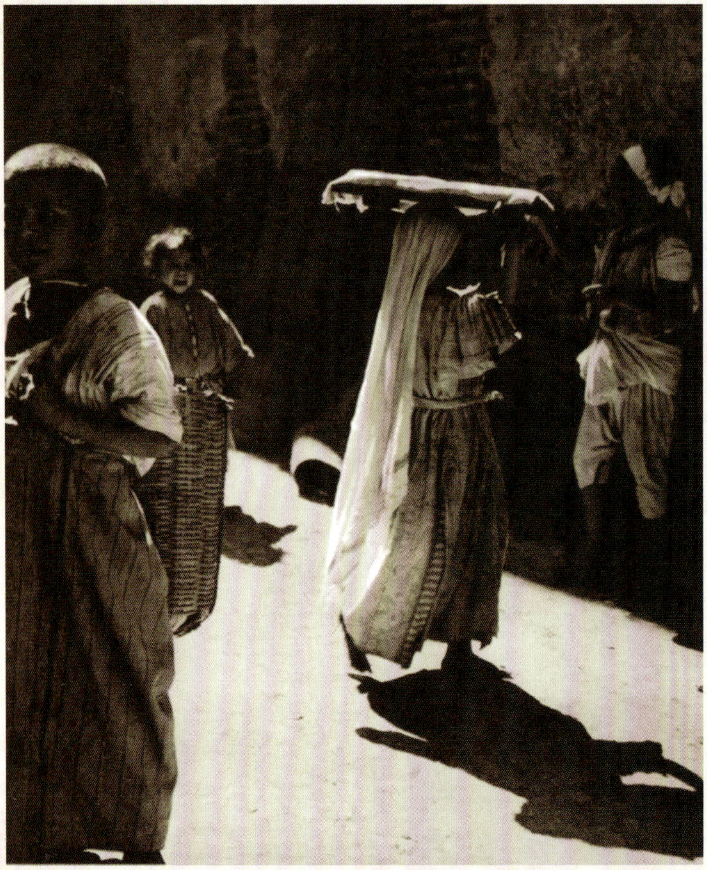
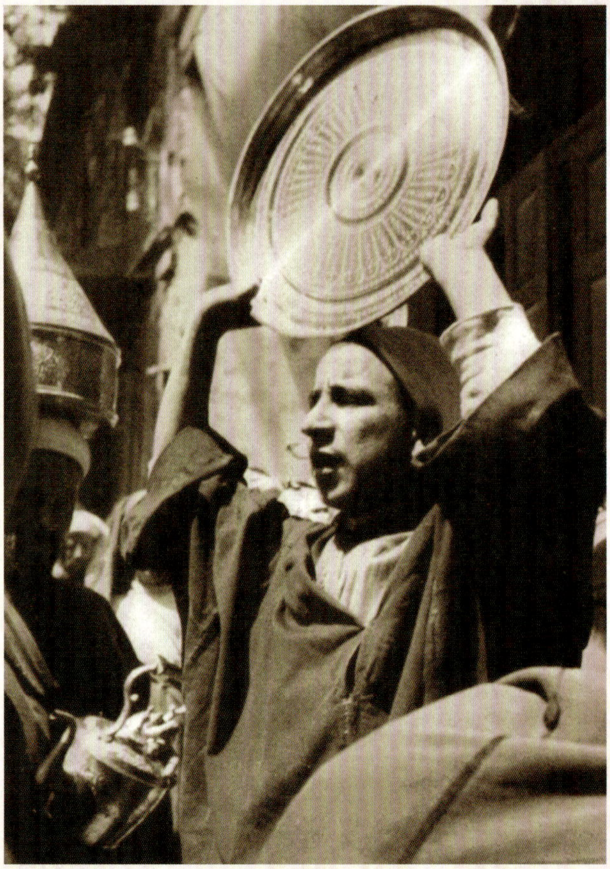

Chapter 2

Saving the Medina

As we approach the twelve-hundredth anniversary of the founding of Fez, let us express the wish that decisive steps will be taken to save the medina. No other city in the entire Arab world manifests so homogeneously what one could call Islamic urbanism. Indeed, one must go to Asia—to Isfahan or Herat—to find other examples as pure and complete as Fez.

While the historical interest of a city like old Fez is irrefutable, some will tell us, one still cannot prevent a city from developing over time and, consequently, from shedding its medieval aspect. A city is not built primarily for tourists and historians, but for the people who live in it, and it should meet their needs. When these change, the city will also change, according to a simply natural law. May the most precious of its historical monuments be preserved to the extent possible, without jeopardizing its development, and as for the rest, let things take their course . . .

This argument would be valid for a city developing in a normal fashion towards more open and flexible forms, thereby better adapting itself to new demands. But nothing of the sort is happening. The Fez medina is becoming ever more densely coagulated, like some cancerous body with cells multiplying to excess. In this situation, "letting things take their course" means letting the medina destroy itself. The longer one waits, the more brutal the means to relieve the situation will be. Meanwhile, the historic and artistic quality of the city will undergo great damage, since this quality lies less in certain details than in the overall image, an image which makes Fez the most beautiful example of Arabo-Islamic urbanism as well as the purest and most homogeneous legacy of the so-called "Hispano-Moorish" civilization, which in reality is that of the entire Maghrib al-Aqṣā ("Far West"), including formerly Arab Andalusia. The disappearance or the decomposition of the old city of Fez would be a very serious loss, not only for Morocco and for international tourism, but for the whole world; one of the last remaining bridges between the current world and that of Islam at its medieval apogee would be destroyed forever.

The French occupiers certainly recognized the value of the medina, and it was upon their example that a series of Sharīfian decrees were promulgated protecting the city's monuments, including its ramparts and even its general character. These decrees are still in effect and have had the merit of preserving the entire old town; that is, until recently when events began to outstrip them. They became insufficient—as we are obliged to note—doubtless because their application was based on an overly static concept of the city, which little by little, came to be regarded more as a museum than as a living organism. It is, however, no longer possible to isolate the preservation of architectural patrimony from broader issues of town-planning. In Europe, the restoration of old towns undertaken since the last world war has shown us that one cannot truly preserve a historical monument without preserving the environment whereof it forms an organic part, and that this environment can be kept

Opposite top left: Berber family from the Rif settled in Fez; *Top right*: Berber youth in a *funduq*; *Bottom left*: Girl carrying unbaked bread to a communal oven; *Bottom right*: Merchant in the copper market

alive only if one can guarantee the conditions whereon it naturally depends. A building such as the grand Qarawiyīn Mosque, for example, would not be what it is if, instead of being surrounded by narrow streets, it were lined with motorways. Not only would such a change destroy the fascinating contrast between the chiaroscuro maze of the souks and the vast space of the mosque opening onto its inner courtyard, but also, on a communal level, the mosque would lose its character as an inviolable and imperturbable refuge in the very heart of the city.

Fortunately it is still possible to prevent the mortal degradation of the Fez medina by strengthening everything that contributes to its normal equilibrium. One of the factors of equilibrium is precisely the existence of those openings onto the sky that are the inner courtyards and enclosed gardens, the *riyāḍ*. Together they form the city's true lungs, given that Arab houses do not open out onto the streets and that the latter are so made as to give hardly any air or light to the dwellings.[1] A house of this type suits the climate, and, in particular, the summer climate when Fez becomes a Saharan city. The inner courtyard collects the relatively cold air which descends into it at night, while the hot daytime air flows over this well of coolness. Fāssī houses are far less comfortable in winter, but the citizens were in the habit of occupying the upper stories during the cold season and the ground floor during times of intense heat. A house with a patio undoubtedly protects the inhabitants from dust and heat, but it also expresses, through its introverted form, the Islamic conception of familial life. The latter is withdrawn from the outer world, from the world of traffic and combat; its intimacy is inviolable, sacred (*ḥarām*).

In the same order of things, it is necessary to point out the separation that exists between the residential quarters of Fez and its trade quarters or souks, a separation common in Islamic cities. Souks are usually located along main transport thoroughfares and towards the town center, whereas residential areas willingly turn away from these same thoroughfares and spread out towards the periphery of the city. The small streets crossing the main thoroughfares to provide access to the houses are effectively only alleyways—their narrowness discouraging traffic rather than inviting it. Here again, the layout of an Islamic city resolves in advance a problem that preoccupies modern town-planners: how to separate, without completely disassociating, the commercial and residential quarters.

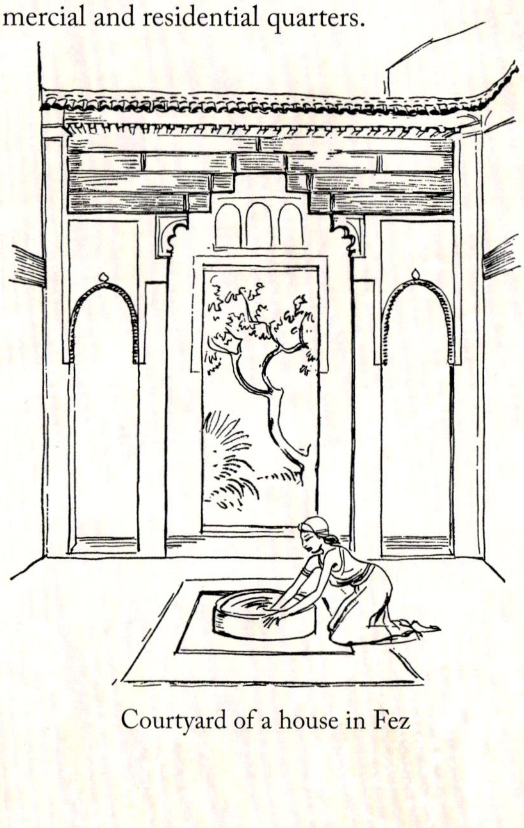

Courtyard of a house in Fez

[1] Furthermore, it would be a serious mistake to adopt the European system of dwellings looking out onto a street open to vehicles, when the great problem of modern town-planning is protecting houses from polluted air and the traffic noise.

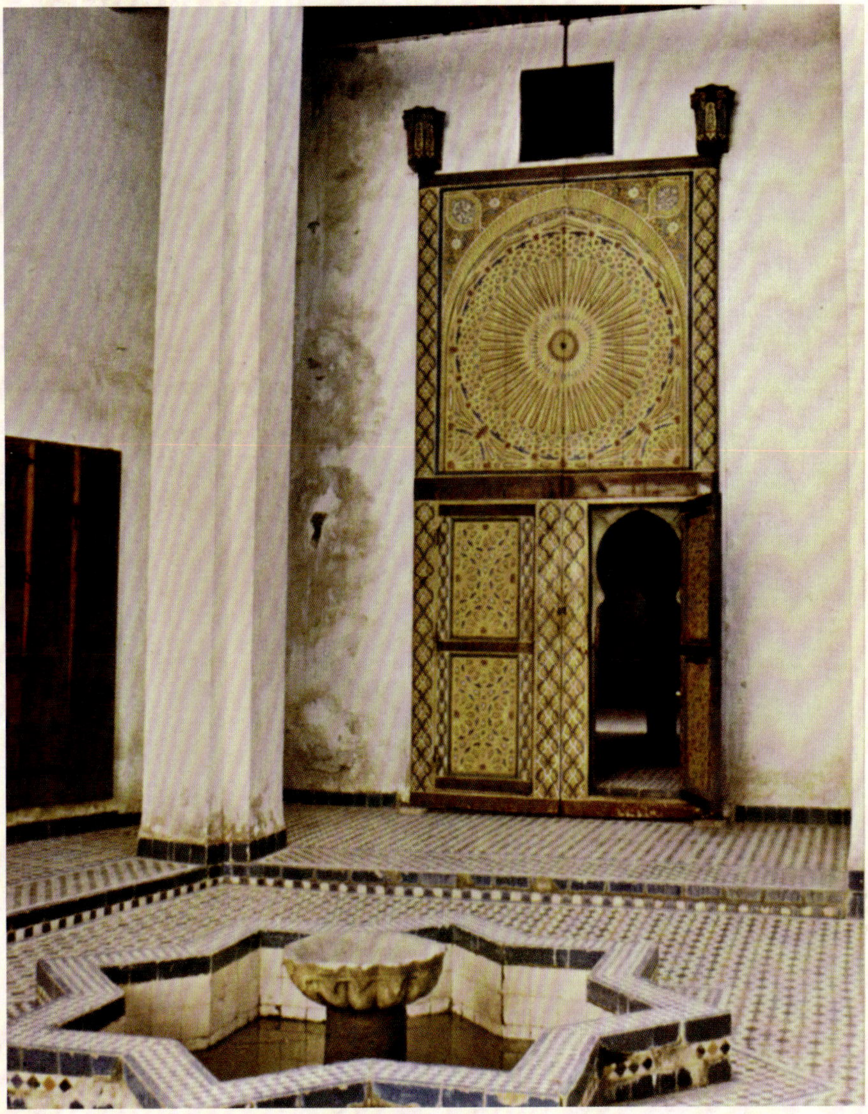

Courtyard with fountain in the former royal palace of Dār al-Baṭḥā

But let us return to the patios, whose walls are like the interior façades of Fāssī houses. Many patios are veritable works of art. By protecting them, we preserve not only a vital element of the city but also artistic treasures that are not necessarily destined to remain hidden treasures, for it is desirable that the most threatened of these patios should soon become public possessions. In the Fez medina at present there are private palaces falling into ruin. Their rehabilitation would certainly not cost more than the construction of new cultural and artistic centers outside of the old town.

Citizens of the old class who have remained faithful to the medina provide an important guarantee of equilibrium. Among them are numerous craftsmen, some of whom work for tourism, while others have preserved a Moroccan clientele, urban or rural. These

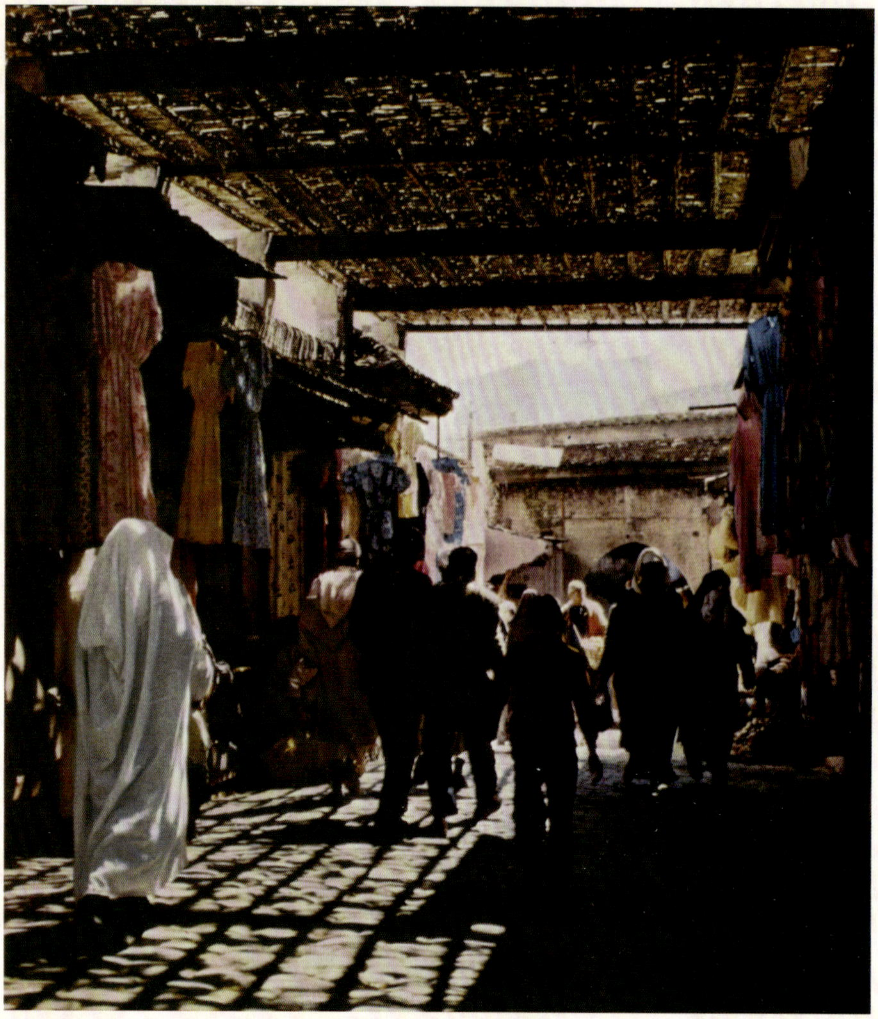

Entrance to a market in Fez

craftsmen—whether they produce tea trays, tables, wooden ploughs, or even embroidered leather—represent an element of stability because, in contrast to the rural workforce living in the medina but normally working elsewhere, they have the possibility and privilege of living and working in place. One would thus not want these craftsmen to be attracted to new centers located outside the medina, except perhaps for some of them such as the potters and the tanners who, in the over-crowded town, no longer find large enough spaces for their equipment.

Through wisdom and prudence, Fez has never easily opened its heart. In some places, the streets are covered with reed awnings, lined with shops, and resemble rooms more than streets. In other places, the passageways are straight and barren until suddenly widening into small squares onto which the portals of mosques open. Mention must be made, however, of the cut into the medina that was made along the Wādī Abū al-Khararīb. This *wādī* having become a foul-smelling drain because

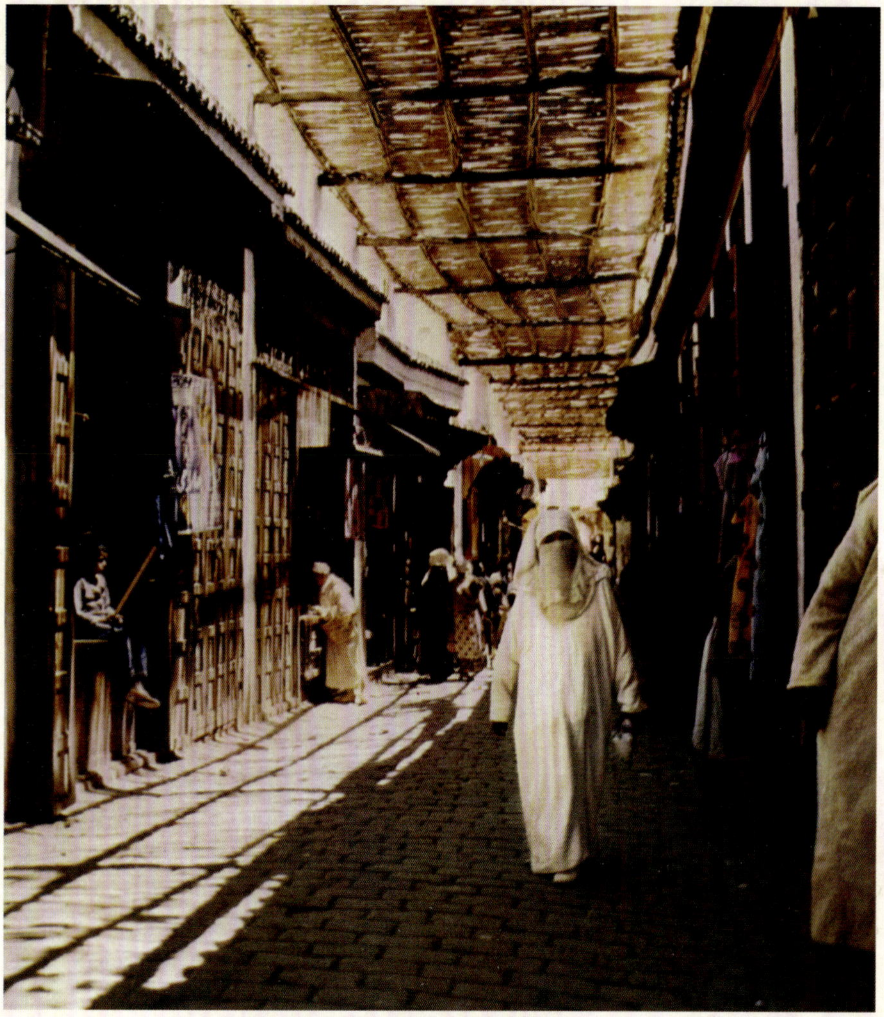

Qīsāriyyah, the central marketplace in Fez

of the growing urban population and perhaps also because of a decrease in the river's flow due to upstream water consumption, it was decided to cover it over and build a motorway on top of it. The project dates from the period of the French Protectorate,[2] though its fulfillment fell during the years 1961 to 1968. The *wādī* was covered over starting from where it comes into the town, but without continuing all the way to where it leaves it, ending instead not far from the center; very fortunately as it happens, for a motorway crossing the entire town with its continuous transit traffic would have practically speaking cut it into two. The river bed being of insufficient width for a road, it was necessary to pull down a large number of houses on both banks. This now opens up the most sheltered and most secret neighborhood of Fez, which not without reason bears the name of *mukhfiyyah* (hidden), and closely borders the center of the old town; even today the Abū al-Kharārīb road still gives the impression of a bombed or earthquake-stricken site.

[2] The period of the French Protectorate was from 1912-1956. —Editors' Note

For tourists who visit Fez, the old thoroughfares—the two Tala'as, the route going down from Bāb al-Jīssah, and the one coming up from Bāb al-Futūḥ and going by the al-'Andalūs Mosque—remain the most fascinating with their twists and turns and covered passageways. The approach by the Abū al-Kharārīb route does not offer the same surprises; it is even likely to be quite disappointing given the chaotic aspect of the partially destroyed houses surrounding the breech. Even if restored, the houses would never again form an organic profile; it would be best to hide them with a screen of trees planted on the two sides of the now covered-over river. There will always be an open perspective on the surprising mass of houses on the Rās Sharāṭīn side.

This gash in the landscape can be likened to a surgical procedure undertaken after all hope of a normal cure has been abandoned, the patient being the over-populated old town. The operation, although painful, was successful in the sense that the new route has been able to take part of the load off of old, overly frequented transport routes, and does not seem, for the moment, to have had such ill effects as disrupting the marketplaces of the medina. The danger persists, however, for it is to be feared that motorized transport coming so close to the town center may well introduce forms of commerce which are incompatible with traditional markets, such as large retail stores monopolizing the sale of certain basic commodities or industrial articles.

Apart from a few inconveniences, such as the rarity of places where one can sit and refresh oneself, the Fez medina is best experienced on foot. The medina fascinates foreign visitors in part by the richness of its architectural values but even more so by the fact that the rhythm of life in the medina is in perfect harmony with the architectural scene. The great genius not easily found elsewhere is this unity of art and life. In view of the advantages that well organized "cultural tourism" can bring to it, Fez has every interest in forbidding motorized traffic. We may dare to hope that the breech at Abū al-Kharārīb will suffice to ensure access to provisions.[3]

Since the beginning of the twentieth century, five different calamities have struck the old city of Fez. The first, due to the government of the Protectorate, was the transfer of the country's capital from Fez to Rabat. In one stroke, Fez was deprived of an elite class of citizens, both the high-ranking officials who followed the court, and the wealthy merchants who settled in Rabat and Casablanca since the maritime trade routes then became more important than the overland routes across the country. This calamity is irreversible in itself, but could be compensated by something else, notably by a revival of Islamic learning in the environment of old Fez—for Fez remains *in potentia* the spiritual capital of Morocco.

A second calamity, which occurred shortly after Morocco's independence,[4] was the transfer of the teaching staff of the ancient university-mosque of al-Qarawiyīn to a site outside the old town walls. Whatever pedagogical and other reasons may have determined this change, the fact remains that the city lost its intellectual center, a center which radiated not

[3] Another cut is planned from an already existing breech at the foot of the hill from which the northern *burj* (tower) rises. But this cut will demand expropriations so massive and costly that we do not believe it will be useful. All roads suitable for motor vehicles that the authorities wish to be built through the medina will be immediately invaded by intense motorized traffic. This traffic will only continue to increase, yet without ever sufficing to transport all the people who leave the medina in the morning and return in the evening.

[4] Moroccan independence was declared on March 2, 1956. —Editors' Note

only in educational and academic circles, but throughout the entire population. Those who remember the times when the *'ulamā'* still taught in the great mosque, openly and without excluding anyone from listening, know how many common people—craftsmen and small merchants—used to close their shops for an hour or two during the day in order to listen to some illustrious professor commenting on a work of law, of *ḥadīth*, or of *sīrah*! They sat outside the circle of the *ṭullāb* (students) at a respectful distance from the professor, but without missing a word of what he said; many of them were in their own way cultivated in *fiqh* and *adab*. There is a suggestion to resume public courses on *ḥadīth* in the Qarawiyīn Mosque, which would contribute greatly to stabilizing the life of the city, currently turned upside down by demographic growth.

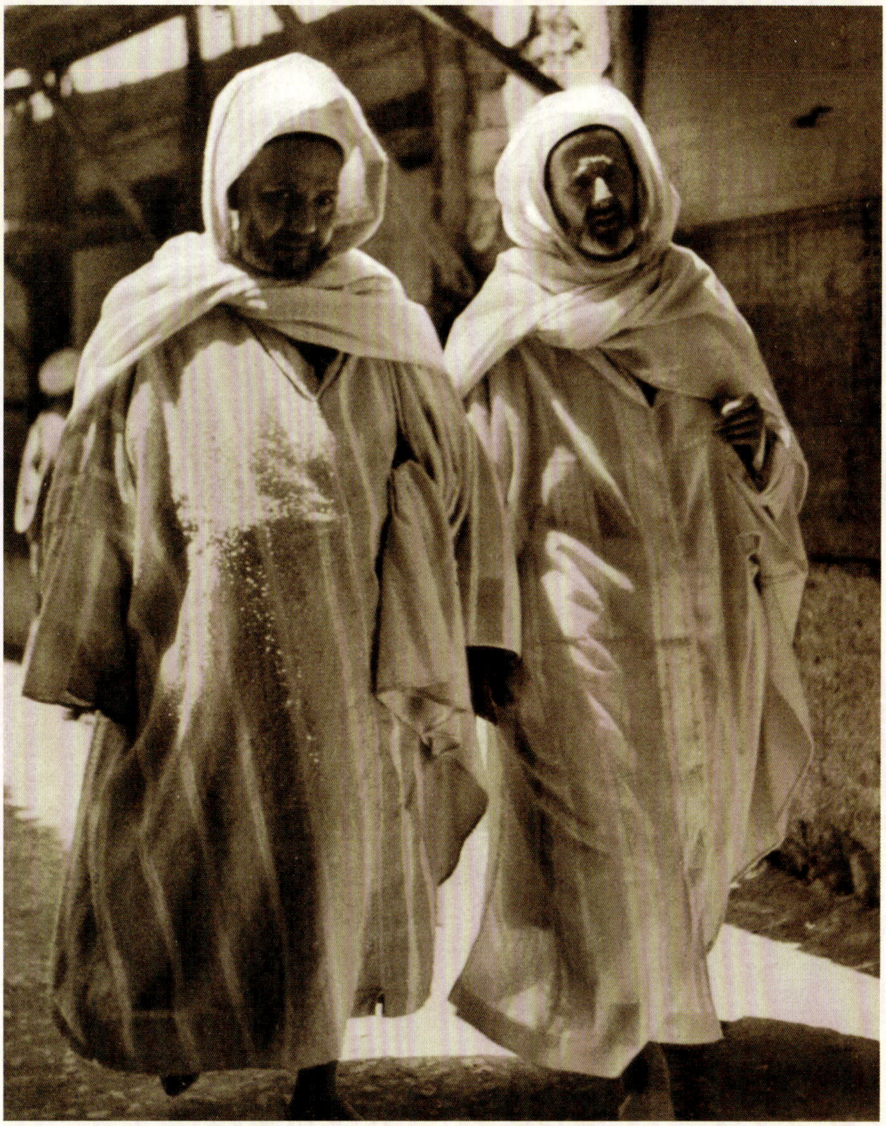

Learned men on their way to al-Qarawiyīn University-Mosque

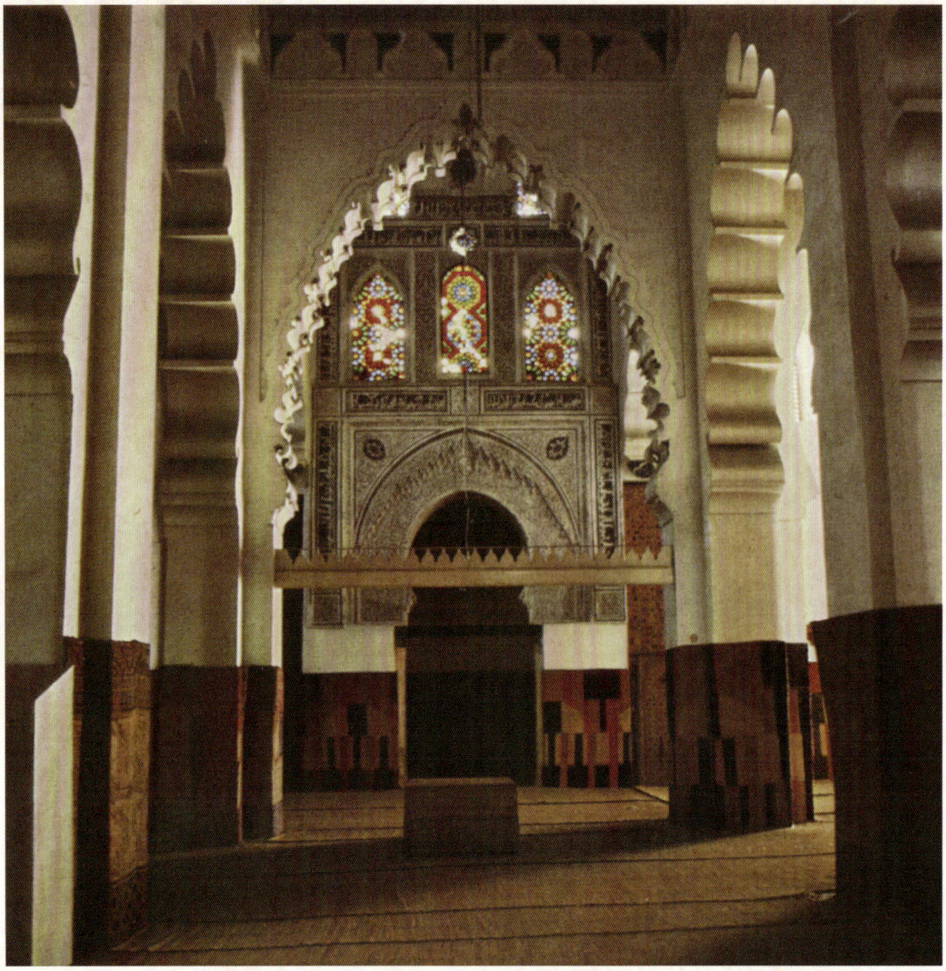

Miḥrāb of al-Qarawiyīn University-Mosque

With the abandonment of the great mosque as a place of learning, the religious colleges also lost their reason for being. As almost all of these *madāris* dated back to the Marinid era (fourteenth century AD) and are generally of great architectural beauty, they were turned into monuments accessible to tourists. This was a way to preserve them, but they are alienated from their true function nonetheless. It would be preferable to see them integrated into life, and one may well ask whether one of them could not serve as an institute for Islamic studies for American and European students, who would probably be happy to live for a semester in this marvelous architectural environment, listening to lessons from some Arab professors. The lessons would focus on classical Arabic, including the reading of fundamental texts on the history of Islam. The higher the level of teaching, the stronger the attraction would be for a certain elite class of Western students, so that there would be no damage to the native environment.

The third calamity, which took place at the same time or a little before, was the banishment of the religious brotherhoods, who were thereby made to pay for the politics

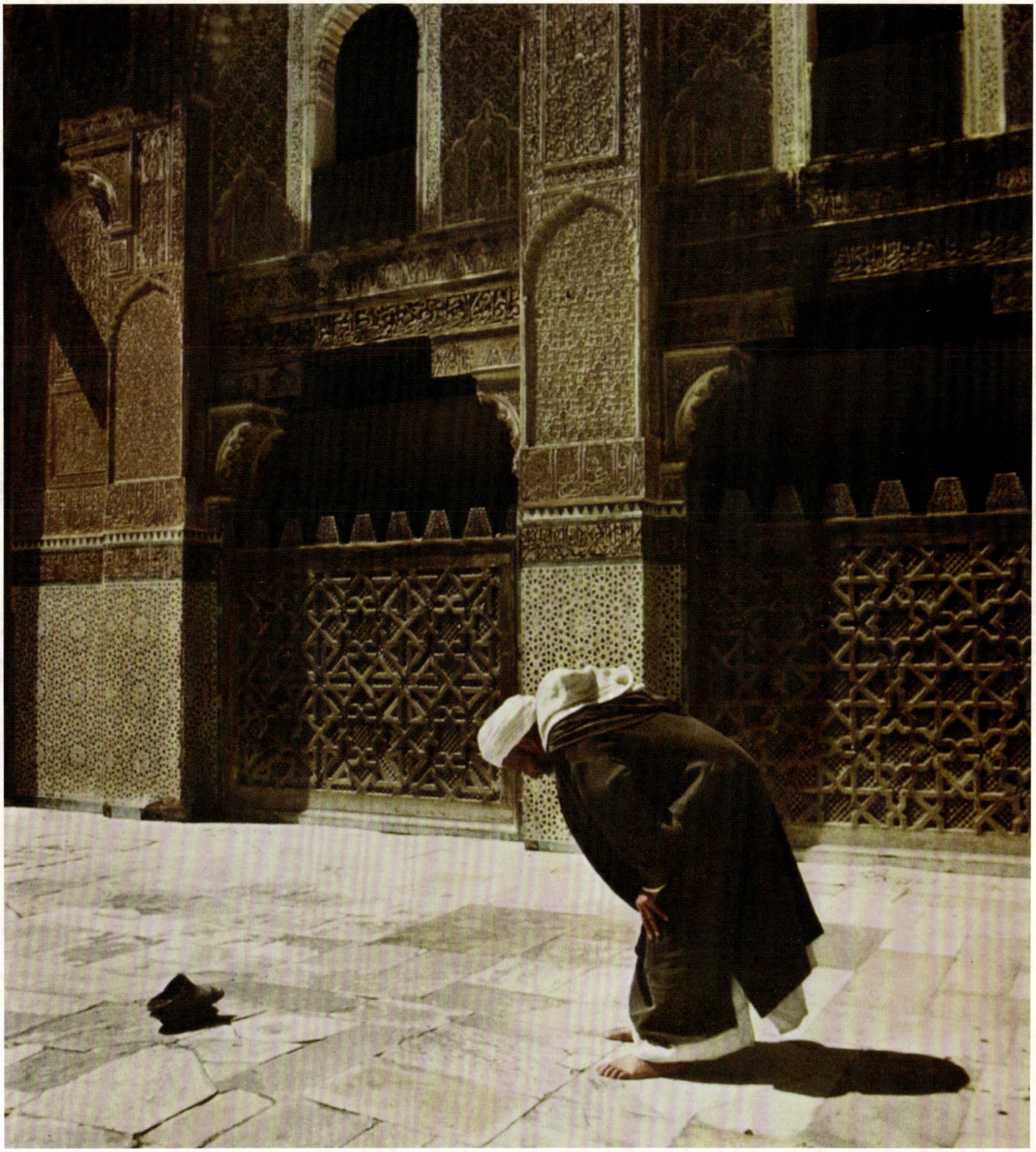

Man praying in the courtyard of Madrasah Bū ʻInāniyah

not of their true spiritual leaders, but of their nominal leaders who had been more or less imposed by the government of the Protectorate. This banishment has not been definitive, but most of the brotherhoods have been unable to return to their former properties in Fez. Now, the beneficial influence that these brotherhoods had on the craft circles is well known. In a general way, they were the inheritors of a wisdom far surpassing the merits or demerits of the individuals who vehicled it.

The decline of the brotherhoods coincides, moreover, with the erosion of the trade guilds, an erosion which in its turn precipitated the decline of the crafts themselves. Craftsmen are losing their principles, their sense of professional honor, and acceding more and more to the compromises suggested by tourism. The only means of slowing this decay is to establish a craft school which would allow qualified representatives of the traditional crafts—the still existing authentic masters—to transmit their knowledge under dignified and favorable circumstances. It is poverty that forces many craftsmen to produce at a level inferior to their qualifications, and this poverty is the result of the fourth great calamity which, alas, we must enumerate.

It consists of the exodus of the majority of the old urban families to the new town[5] or to other towns. This exodus responds to the attraction of the new commercial centers, and is also the result of the sort of fascination exerted by a new way of life with its as-of-yet unexhausted possibilities. The fact that the new town has been the seat of the civil and military authorities, first under the French Protectorate and later under the national government, bestows upon it a special prestige; living in the new city means not only enjoying the frequently dubious conveniences of modern life, it is also a matter of social standing. It is true that the old town of Fez is in certain respects uncomfortable: the houses are cold in winter, the streets steep and tiring. These are the endearingly human aspects of the town we readily undervalue when we are used to them. Here, then, is a drama that is writ large in a very general context: the destruction by modern technology of ways of life which are comparatively simple at the material level whatever their virtues at other levels. This process unfolds in a single direction, not because the nature of things demands it—progress, even limited to its most exterior aspects, is not always rational—but because a certain prejudice would have it so.

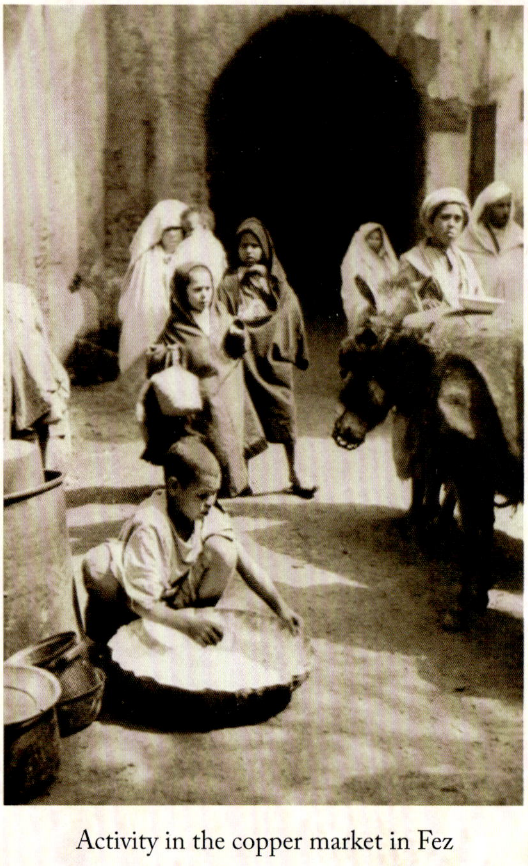

Activity in the copper market in Fez

[5] The modern city of Fez, the Ville Nouvelle, was founded by Marshal Lyautey in 1916 and is located to the south-west of the old city of Fez (Fās al-Bāli). It is to be distinguished from Fās al-Jādīd ("New Fez"), the medieval royal city founded by the Marinids in the fourteenth century. —Editors' Note

When the exodus under discussion began, the Fez medina was in no wise uninhabitable. It risks, however, becoming so due to this very exodus, for the fourth calamity gave rise to the fifth, namely the massive immigration of country folk in search of work. This immigration has invaded even the smallest habitable spaces, filling up the available houses beyond all normal measure, and simultaneously giving rise to a widespread real-estate speculation that threatens to transform Fez into a massive dormitory. Moroccan houses with their patio that can be made into an enclosed garden, are made for a single family. Families may be made up of several generations but they constitute an autonomous world. When overpopulation forces several families—up to twenty in an average house—to live around the same courtyard, traditional architecture loses its meaning. Sacred intimacy is replaced by a degrading and impoverished promiscuity.

Given this situation, anything that increases the population density is an evil: the construction of new houses inside the medina, the use of *fanādiq* as lodging for country folk in search of work, and, above all, the partitioning of houses, palaces, and gardens abandoned by their former owners—all of this contributes

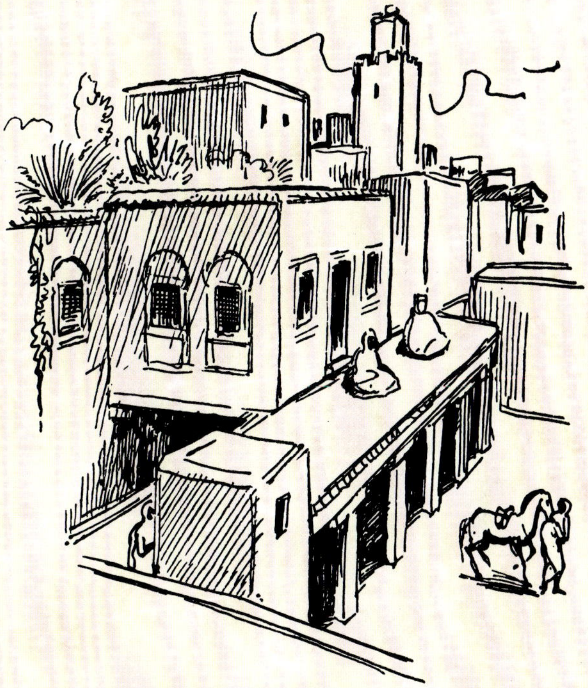

Above and below:
Drawing and plan of a *riyāḍ* in Fez

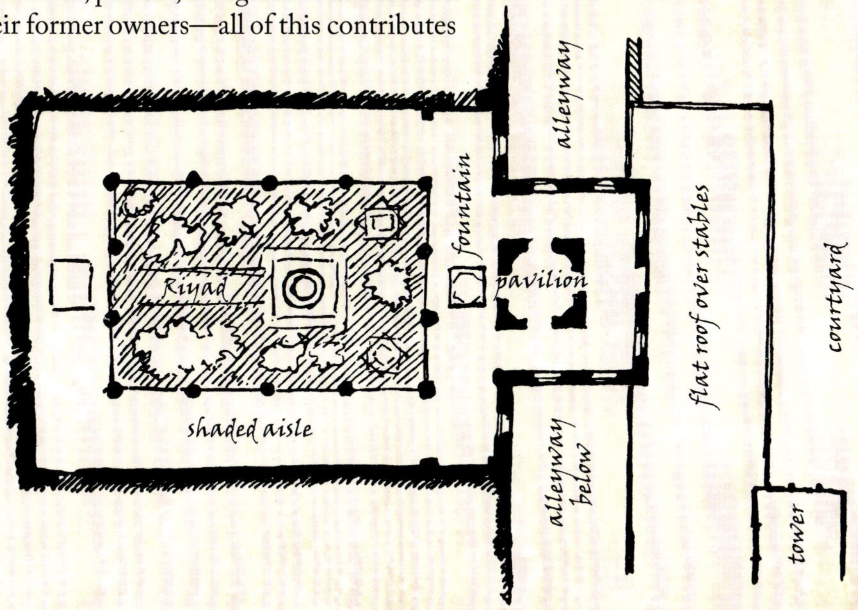

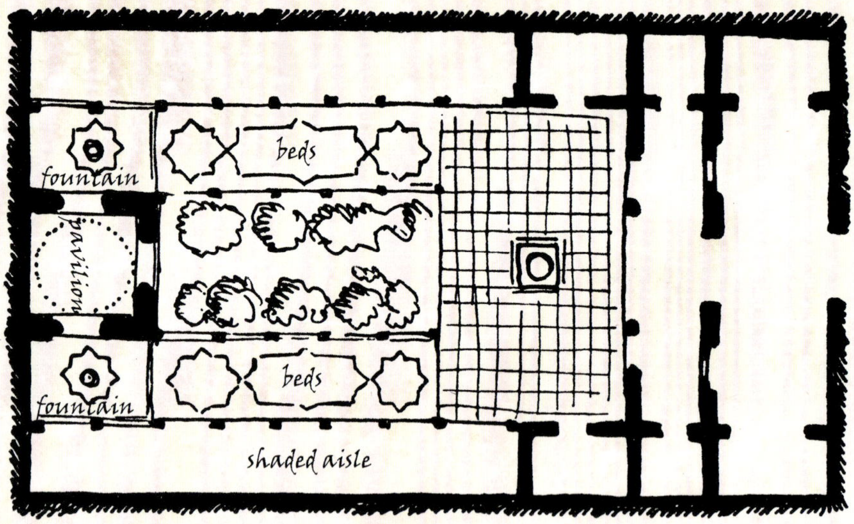

Plan of a garden

to the city's suffocation.[6] And the worst is that this development trend risks being irreversible: once transformed into tenement housing, these great houses can never be restored. At the same time, the density of the population is increasing dangerously beyond what the traditional town structure is able to assimilate.

Let us specify that the immigration of rural elements is not an evil in itself, and has always existed to a certain extent. What is much worse than ever before is their exploitation by landlords. The latter make the excuse that maintenance of these great houses has become overly burdensome and they are more or less obliged to rent them by pieces. The result is no less catastrophic: things are continuing as if it were a matter of proving that the Fez medina has become uninhabitable—it is being abandoned to the poor who have no other choice.

To alleviate the pressure on the medina, new reception centers for country migrants need to be created outside the medina, which will require great effort on the part of the responsible authorities. At the same time, new centers of artistic and intellectual life should be set up in the old town, while respecting as far as possible its own traditions. Ultimately, success will depend upon the power of regeneration inherent to its traditions or to tradition as such.

Finally, we must point out that Moroccans who have grown up in a more or less traditional setting easily underestimate the persuasive and revelatory power that the ambience of the Fez medina has for a non-Moroccan. We speak of persuasive power because this ambience still represents in principle a perfectly homogeneous world, even though entirely different from that of modern Europe. At the same time, we can speak of a revelatory power because this ambience expresses, in all its positive qualities, oftentimes forgotten

[6] The compact grouping of houses in the old neighborhoods was compensated not only by the existence of inner courtyards, but also by gardens which, until relatively recent times, were spread out between the core of the city and its ramparts. The partitioning of many of these gardens into housing lots was a social charity in appearance only. By offering possibilities of housing to a certain number of people, life was rendered at the same time more difficult for the entire population.

spiritual values. For Moroccans, this is all taken for granted; but to the extent that Moroccans of the younger generation are deepening their experience of the European intellectual world and at the same time distancing themselves from their native environment, the irreplaceable human character of a city like old Fez will become evident. We do not know when the "return to origins" will happen in this country, but it will certainly take place, and it would be a great pity if the image of old Fez—Fās al-Bāli, the city bearing so much of the light of Islam—were to disintegrate in the meantime.

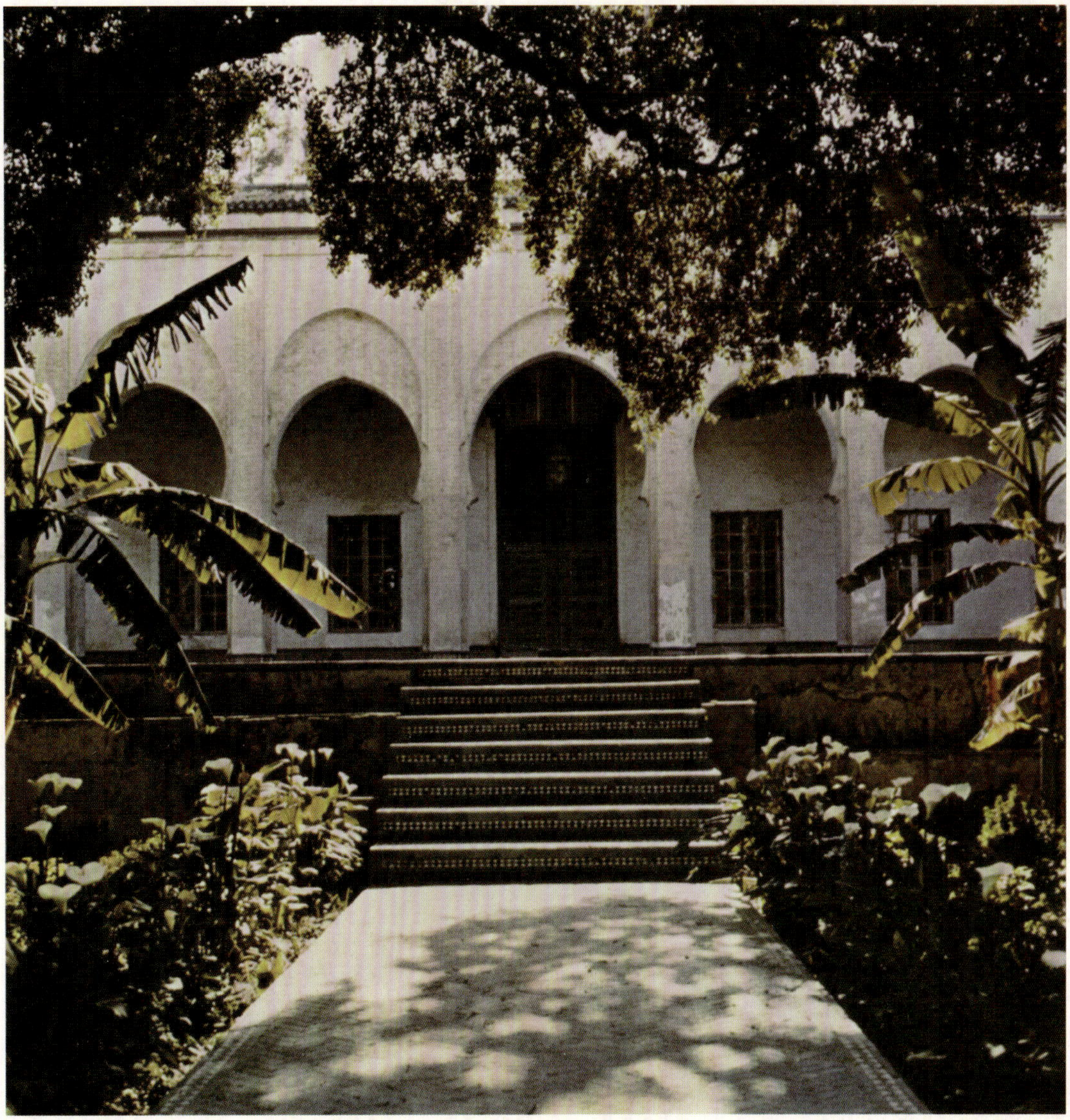

Interior garden in the former royal palace of Dār al-Baṭḥā

II

A Living Heritage

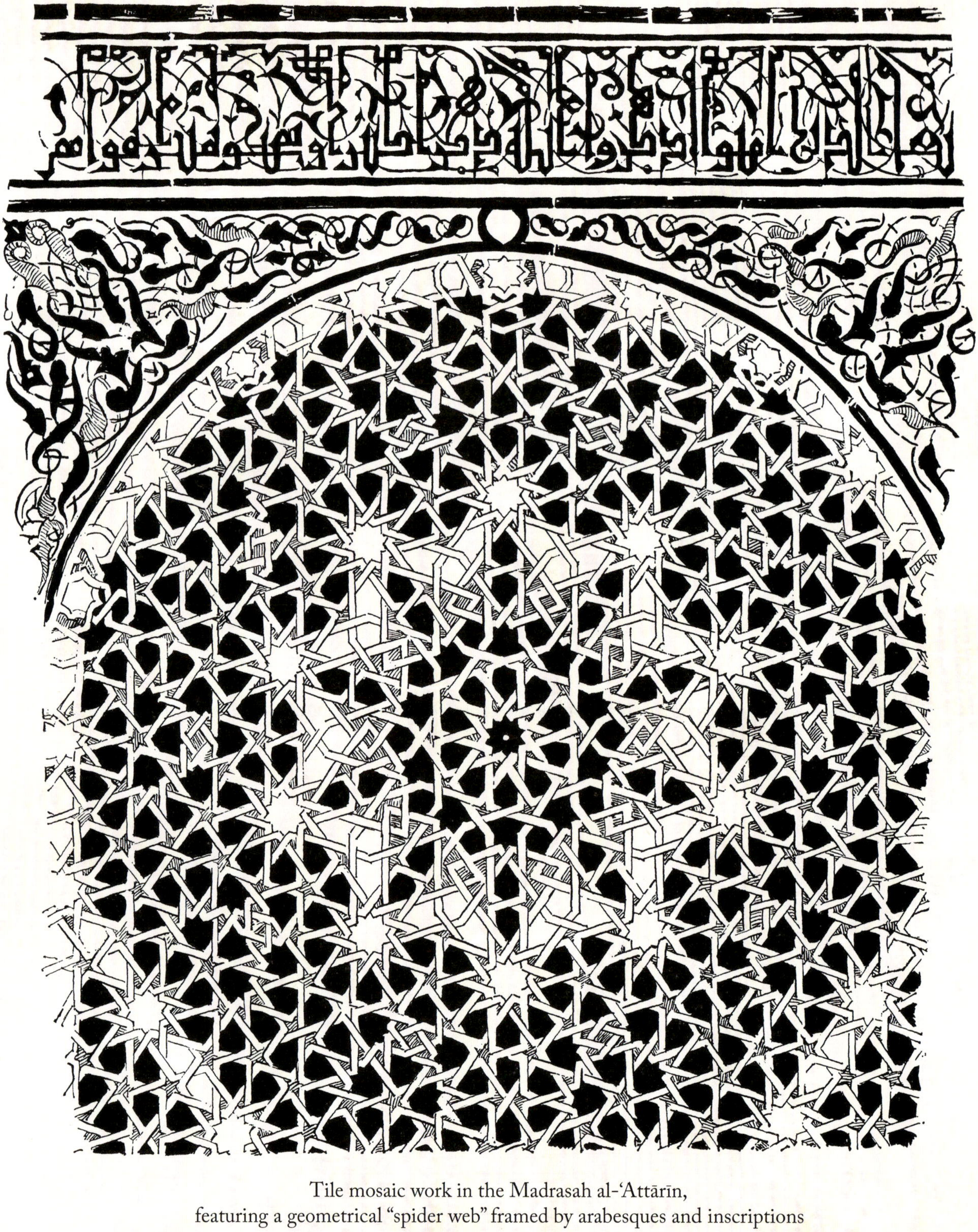

Tile mosaic work in the Madrasah al-'Attārīn,
featuring a geometrical "spider web" framed by arabesques and inscriptions

Chapter 3

Permanent Values of Maghribi Art

The following considerations refer primarily to Moroccan art, which the author knows best, but they apply in essence to the art of the entire Maghrib. Certain art historians, in discussing Maghribi art of the past three or four centuries, speak of "stagnation," or even of "sterile repetition" or "rigidification." The same criticism, equally ill-considered, has been leveled against Islamic art in general, and we greatly fear lest young Moroccans allow themselves to be impressed with judgments of the sort. There is nothing surprising in this, since the prejudice which claims that an ever-more-rapidly changing modern art is the most normal thing in the world, cannot for that very reason pardon Islamic art for being ever true to itself. What is all too quickly labeled as "stagnation" is in reality a positive quality, namely the awareness of values acquired over the course of a logical and necessary development, values which merely translate into visual forms what Islamic spirituality already contains inwardly in other forms. For every spiritual ideal there exists an optimal expression, at least in a certain ethnic context, and once this expression has been found, there is no ground for replacing it by another.

Let us consider the masterpieces of Moroccan architecture such as the Qarawiyīn Mosque in Fez, the Kutubiyyah Mosque in Marrakesh, or the great mosque of Salé, buildings which date, not coincidentally, from the great sixth and seventh centuries of the Hijrah.[1] Who could dispute that they perfectly manifest the spirit of Islam, while responding to the disposition of soul of a people whose roots are both Arab and Berber? Now, neither Islam, nor this ethnic heritage, has changed. Moreover, it suffices to understand the artistic intention inherent in these masterpieces to have the desire to continue this style. We do not say that it is necessary to repeat "word-for-word" the models in question; for servile and unintelligent copying is not a true continuation of an art, nor does it constitute traditional art. The latter requires above all the comprehension of the principles governing a certain art or a certain style; to understand them is to know how to apply them to the always new conditions presented by each task. The mastery of an art is like the mastery of a language: one does not improvise the rules of discourse, and he who uses them willy-nilly is not more liberated, but much more limited, in his expression than he who uses them correctly. We must recall this simple truth because so many false artists of nowadays believe themselves able to invent a new language, to create a new art from nothing. Just as the genius of a language surpasses the individual who speaks it—or let us say that it gives his spirit wings—so too does traditional art surpass, in its essence, the particular artist. This tradition plunges its roots not only into the historical patrimony of an entire people, but also, and what is more, into the timeless spirit of Islam; it lends to the artist the elements of a true language, enabling a simple craftsman, a *mu'allim* without Michelangelesque talents, to create works wherein the soul can quench its thirst for peace and beauty without ever growing weary.

[1] The eleventh and twelfth centuries AD.—Editors' Note

Is what we have just said true only for religious art? Should we apply other measures to profane art? But, in fact, there is no profane art in the framework of Islamic civilization, which admits of no scission between the domains of the "sacred" and the "profane"; there exists, at most, a difference of degrees between an art directly attached to religion, such as the architecture of mosques, for example, and an art of relatively worldly use, such as the architecture of palaces. Let us recall that every Muslim home is in principle a mosque, a *masjid*, that is to say a place where one can accomplish communal rites, a possibility never belied by the traditional house's architectural forms or decoration. In Moroccan or Maghribi art, nothing is truly profane except a work that is deliberately situated outside the Islamic framework. Now, this case does not concern us here, since experience shows that an art of this kind always identifies itself, through its tendencies, with modern European art, while keeping only a vague psychic hue of what is Moroccan.

Let us also recall in this context that the Arabic language makes no distinction between art and craftsmanship, and for good reason, since this distinction is only due to the very particular development of European art since the Renaissance. In all traditional civilizations, art is never disassociated from its practical goal, and craftsmanship is never limited to a production deprived of beauty. To reach this debased state industry was required, and with it the machine. Before that era, the most modest trade had its ideal of perfection, a perfection that necessarily implied beauty, in the sense of the Arabic word *iḥsān*, which has precisely the two meanings. A perfection that excludes beauty is not in conformity with the integral nature of man.

The close link between art and craftsmanship fills the Islamic world with beauty. The art of Islam, moreover, is essentially an art of environment: architecture, woodworking, metalworking, ornamentation, and even calligraphy all serve to fashion man's living environment, figurative art being the exception. "God hath created you and what ye make" (*Allāhu khalaqakum wa mā taʿmalūn*), says the Koran (37:96), thereby indicating two phases of Divine creation: a direct creation whose object is man's nature in its totality, and an indirect creation through man, whose object is the latter's environment. In order for man's creative act to be a conscious prolongation of the divine Act, he must confer upon the things he fashions their state of natural perfection. Now, it is precisely this which Islamic art seeks: it confers upon raw material a state of crystalline perfection by using the most simple and direct means, such as the geometrical arrangement of forms and the cladding of surfaces by colored panels or sculptured ornaments which lend to them a luminous vibration. The Muslim artist works like an alchemist who makes gold from base lead.

One can rightly say that, on the whole, the craftsman or the artist never took care to perfect his tools, nor to choose the most durable of materials, at the same time as he applied himself with much zeal and great skill to the perfection of his work.[2] This attitude is explained at least in part by the Muslim's very keen awareness that all things are ephemeral; art always remains something provisional—*kullu man ʿalaihā fān* ("all that is here-below will perish"), says the Koran (55:26)—and its best fruit is the mastery that the craftsman gains over himself. Here we touch upon

[2] Compared with the refinement of the products, the simplicity of the tools is striking; likewise, the quality of the materials used was often humble, though not to say shabby. Of course, gold and silver work also exist, but they are commonly the monopoly of Jewish craftsmen. As for brocade weaving, which demands precious material and an elaborate apparatus, it represents, like luxury book binding, an art developed in the court of princes.

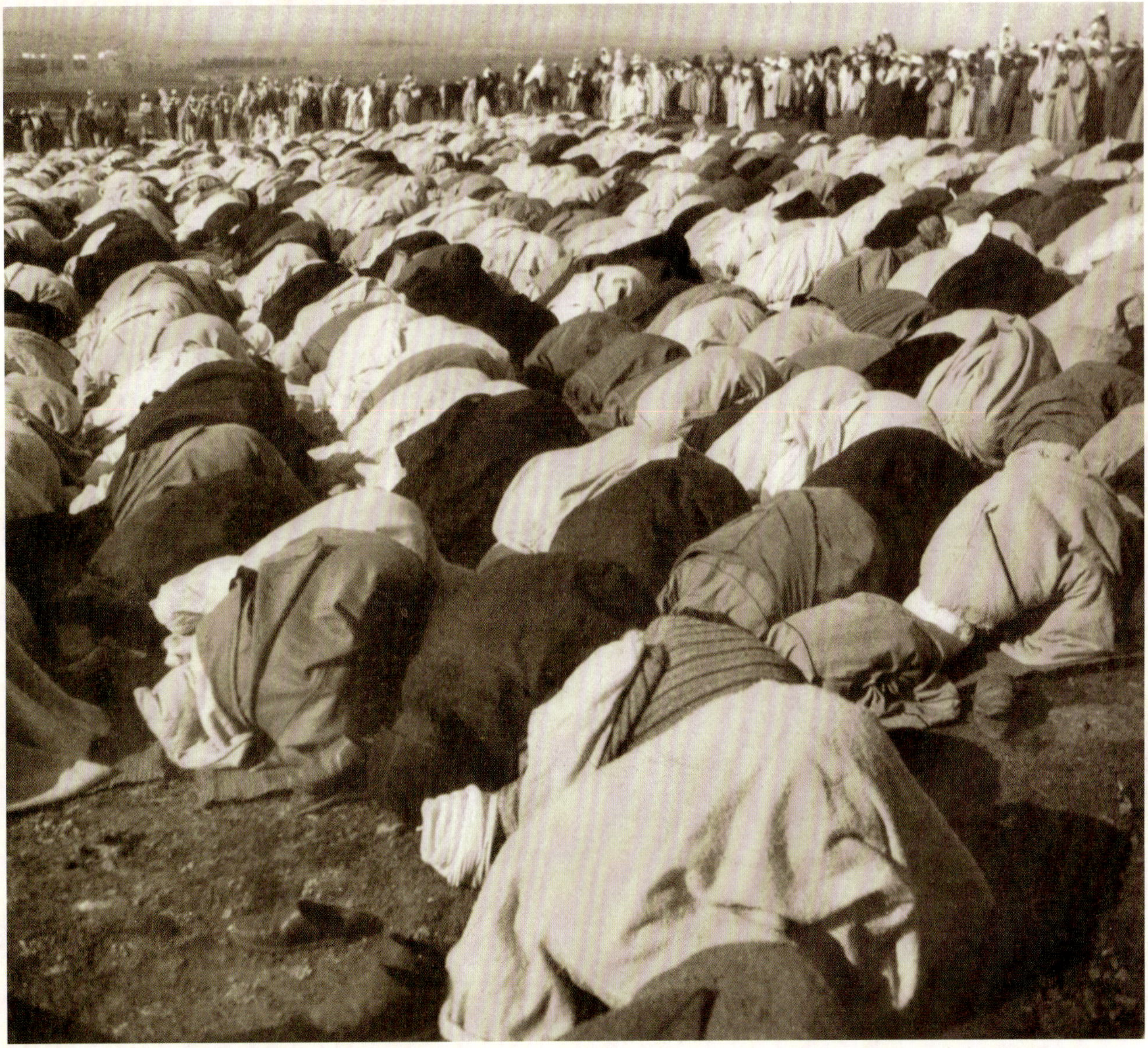

Communal prayer during ʿĪd al-Kabīr in an open field near the town of Mūlay Idrīs

the point where art converges—or can converge—with a spiritual discipline, something which explains the affinity that exists between the craft guilds and the brotherhoods issuing from *taṣawwuf*. In the same way that the craftsman transforms a more or less amorphic or raw material into a perfect and noble form, the contemplative or Sufi transforms his own soul.

One cannot understand typical Moroccan art without situating it within the wider framework of Islamic art, of which it represents a branch determined by a particular ethnic *milieu*, that of the Maghrib in the classical sense of the term, which includes Morocco, Algeria, and the Western part of Tunisia, as

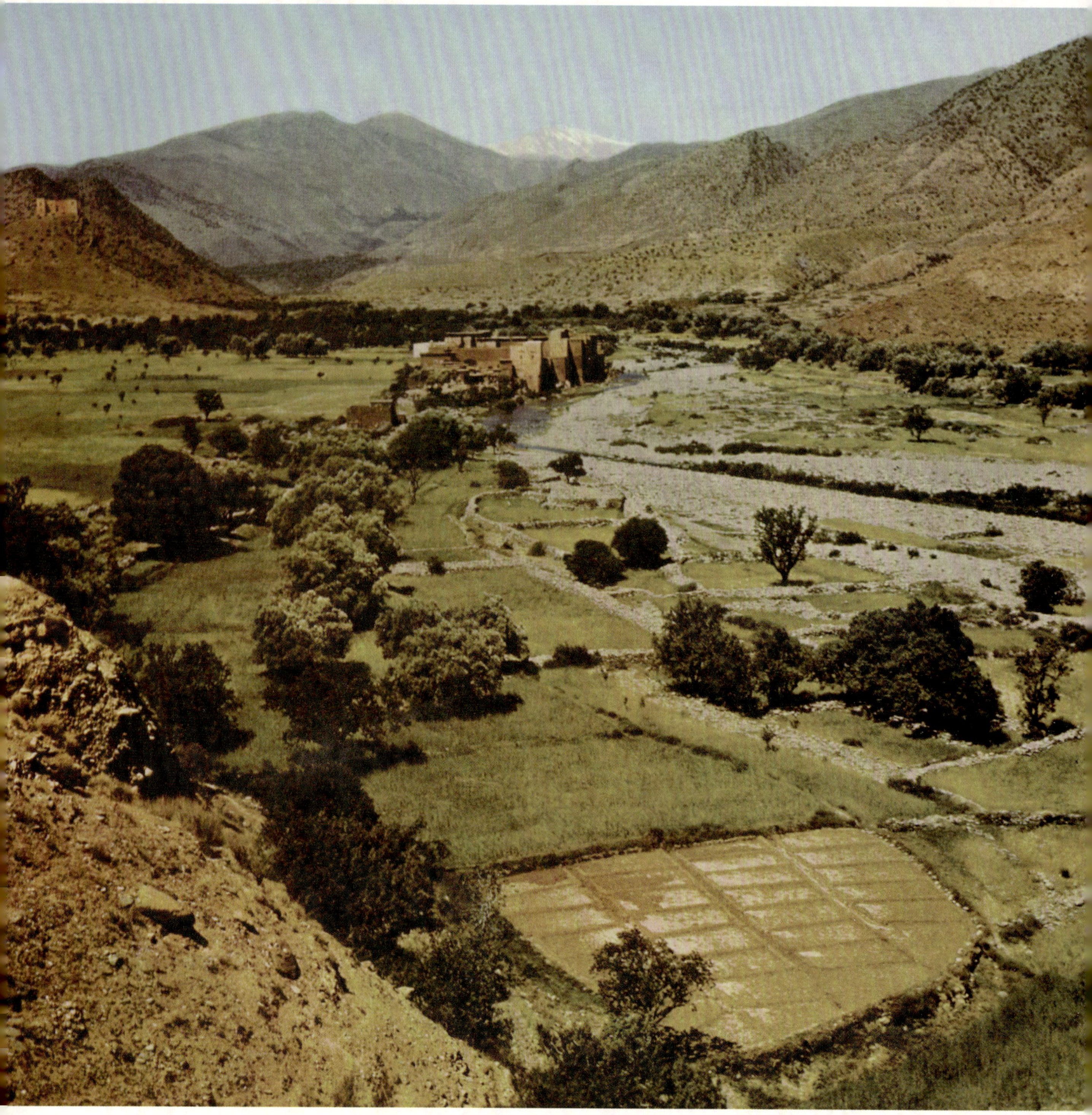

Above: View of the upper N'fīs valley, the area where the Almohad movement began;
Opposite: *Miḥrāb* of the Tīnmal Mosque, built to commemorate the founder of the Almohad dynasty

well as Muslim Spain. Maghribi art went through three principal creative stages, corresponding to the three empires of the Almoravids (*al-Murābiṭūn*), the Almohads (*al-Muwaḥḥidūn*), and the Marinids (*al-Mirīniyūn*).[3] The cultural and artistic unity of this domain was forged by the first two of these great empires, the Almoravids and the Almohads, and by the latter more than the former. In no other moment in Maghribi history have the Berber and Arab heritages been so intimately united, and this is undoubtedly why the artistic synthesis born of this union has been so enduring. Let us note, however, that none of these three creative phases of Maghribi art reacted against a preceding phase in the manner of the European "Renaissance," which rejected the artistic norms of the Middle Ages. In Maghribi art, as in Muslim art in general, the forms of expression created by such-and-such an era overlap peaceably with those of preceding eras, thereby simply enriching the existing vocabulary without ever preventing the artists from returning to an older mode of expression. Fez thus has many relatively recent mosques which in their majesty and sobriety are directly linked to the Almohad heritage.

To define, as is often done, Moroccan art in general and Fāssī art in particular as a provincial variety of Hispano-Moorish art is to forget that the Almoravid and Almohad empires—those most responsible for the cultural unity of the Maghrib—had their center of gravity, not in Spain, but in Morocco; the cultural role of a city like Fez was no more peripheral or "provincial" than that of Granada or Seville. It is also true, however, that the Marinid era, which marked Fez particularly strongly since the Marinid kings resided there,[4] corresponds to the reflux of the cultural heritage of Muslim Spain towards North Africa, and that in many respects Fez is the direct cultural inheritor[5] of the Spain of the Taifas, that is to say, post-caliphal Muslim Spain. The designation of Moroccan art as "Hispano-Moorish" is therefore acceptable, despite seeming to attribute too much importance to Spain, when one notes that Muslim Spain most directly reflected the Arab heritage. In fact, the caliphate of Córdoba, which no longer existed at the time of the great Berber movements just mentioned but whose imprint was still very strong, had jealously preserved its Umayyad (thus Arab and Syrian) heritage, while at the same time also imitating the example of the

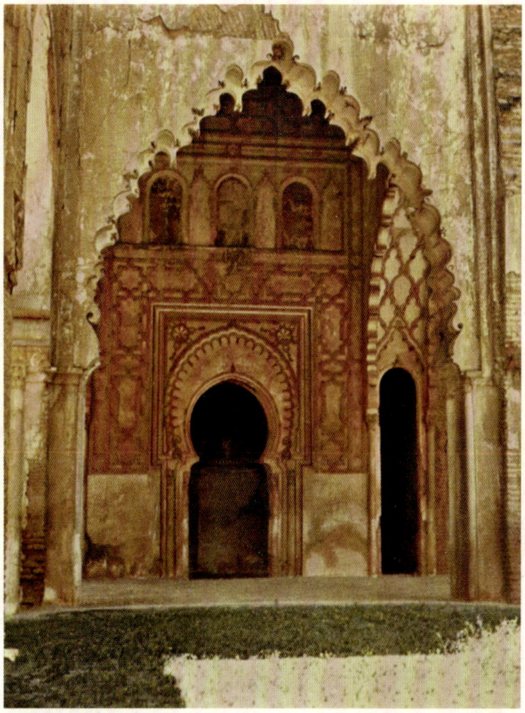

[3] The Almoravid dynasty is usually dated from 1063-1145 AD; the Almohad dynasty from 1121-1269 AD; and the Marinid dynasty from 1244-1465 AD. —Editors' Note

[4] Unlike the Almohad and Almoravid kings, who had their political center in Marrakesh.

[5] A striking example of this direct transmission is the existence in Fez today of "Andalusian" music, which deserves more than a mention in this context.

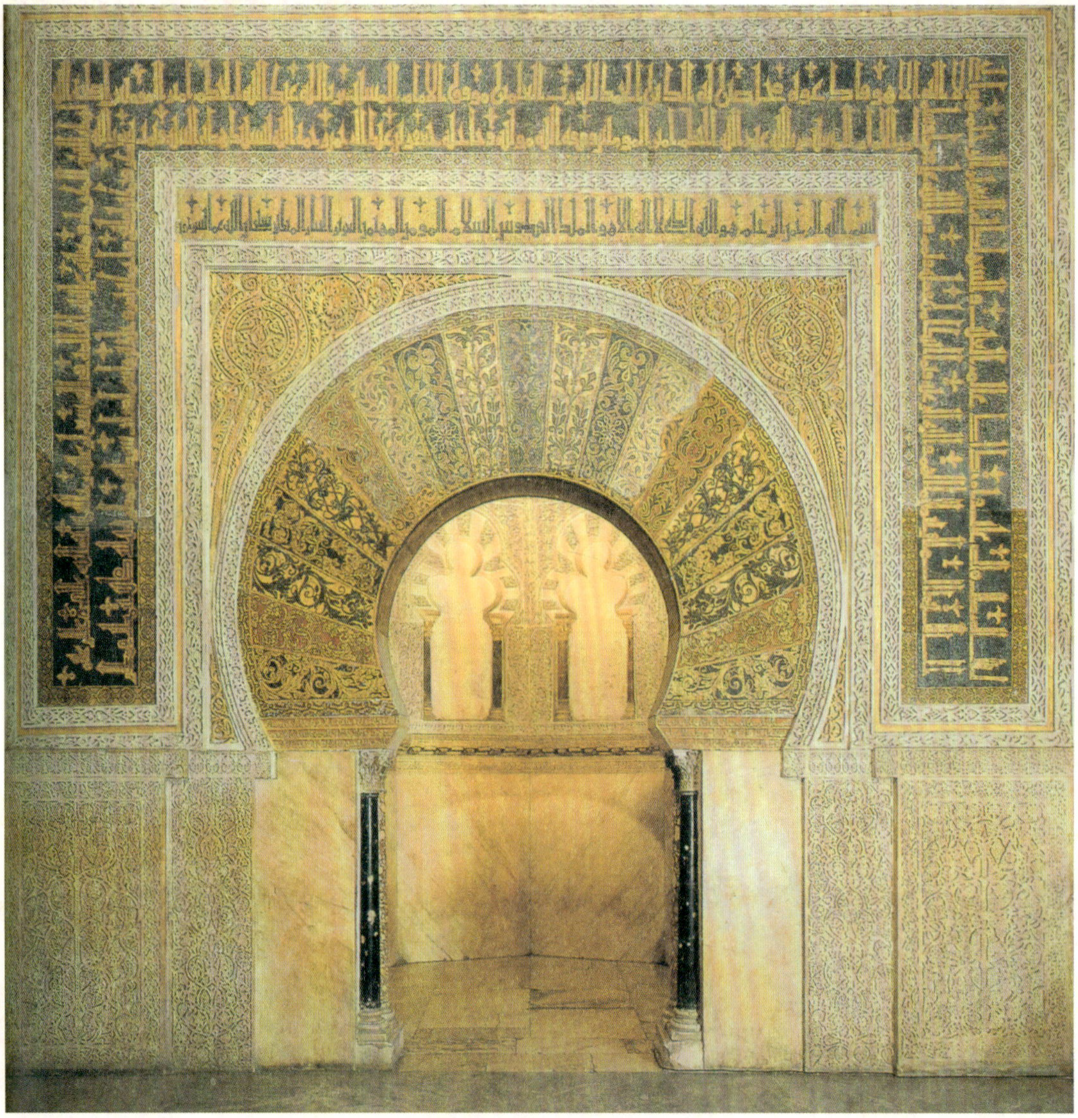

Miḥrāb of the Great Mosque of Córdoba

Abbasids residing in Baghdad. In this way the strongest Arab and Eastern influences rebounded on the Maghrib al-Aqṣā—the Far West, that is to say Morocco—through the intermediary of Spain.

It is for this reason not surprising that one finds in the Umayyad art of Spain forms which are the seeds of what was later developed by Maghribi art. We shall mention here only one example, that of the *miḥrāb* of the Great Mosque of Córdoba. It was built around 965 by Ḥakam II who had master mosaicists come from Constantinople in order to teach their technique to the Muslim craftsmen charged with ornamenting the *miḥrāb*. This technique was not continued in the Maghrib where the mosaic work of colored glass was replaced by that of enameled faience (*zillīj*). As for the ornamental motifs which, in the *miḥrāb* of Córdoba, are still reminiscent of Greco-Roman

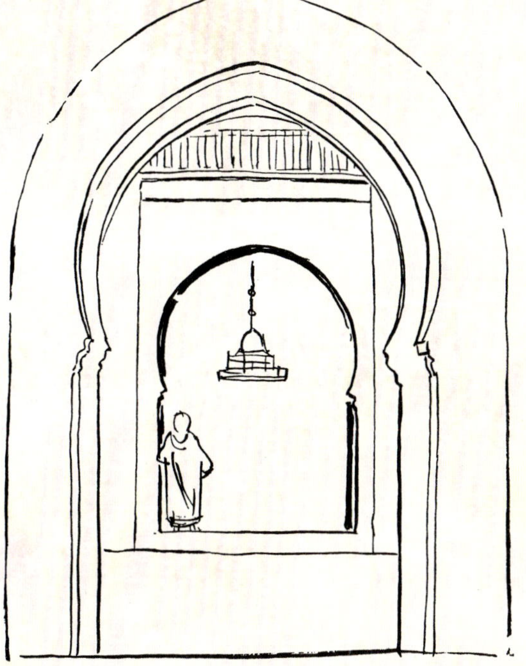

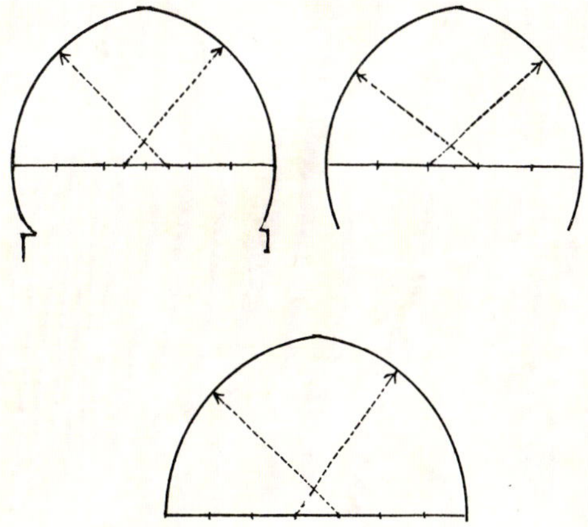

Above and left:
Horseshoe arches with pointed crown

naturalism, they developed in the direction of geometric and rhythmic unity. But it is the general composition of the *miḥrāb* that we wish to consider, for it summarizes in a concise fashion what one might call the secret of Maghribi architecture.

Let us first of all note that the horseshoe arch, such as one finds for example in the Qarawiyīn Mosque, is typical of all Spanish art of the high Middle Ages. It is not known whether the Arabs of Spain received it from the Visigoths or whether they brought it from Syria, but it is certain that the master masons of Córdoba, in setting out their voussoirs in the shape of a fan, gave to it a great expansive strength. One sees the arch dilating from an ungraspable center which, depending on whether one determines it based on the inner or outer profile of the fan of voussoirs, shifts slightly from bottom to top, the result being that the arch appears to rise like the disc of the sun or moon over the horizon. It is an *inshirāḥ*, a beatific dilation, that remains wholly inward because immobilized by the frame. Equilibrium between a dynamic force and static force: herein one finds a concise formula for the composition not only of Maghribi *mahārib*, but of all traditional architecture of the Maghrib.[6] Now equilibrium is an expression of unity, and it is through this that one returns to the very principle of Islam.

The Almohads developed this theme by furnishing the horseshoe arch with a pointed crown, which confers on it something of the ascending movement of a candle's flame. The form of the *miḥrāb*, however, generally preserved the Córdoban model—that of the horseshoe arch whose fanned voussoirs are either nearly or entirely unbroken—just as it preserved the polygonal plan of the niche found first in Córdoba.

[6] In fact, the theme of the radiating arch inscribed within a rectangular frame is typical of the Muslim art of North Africa.

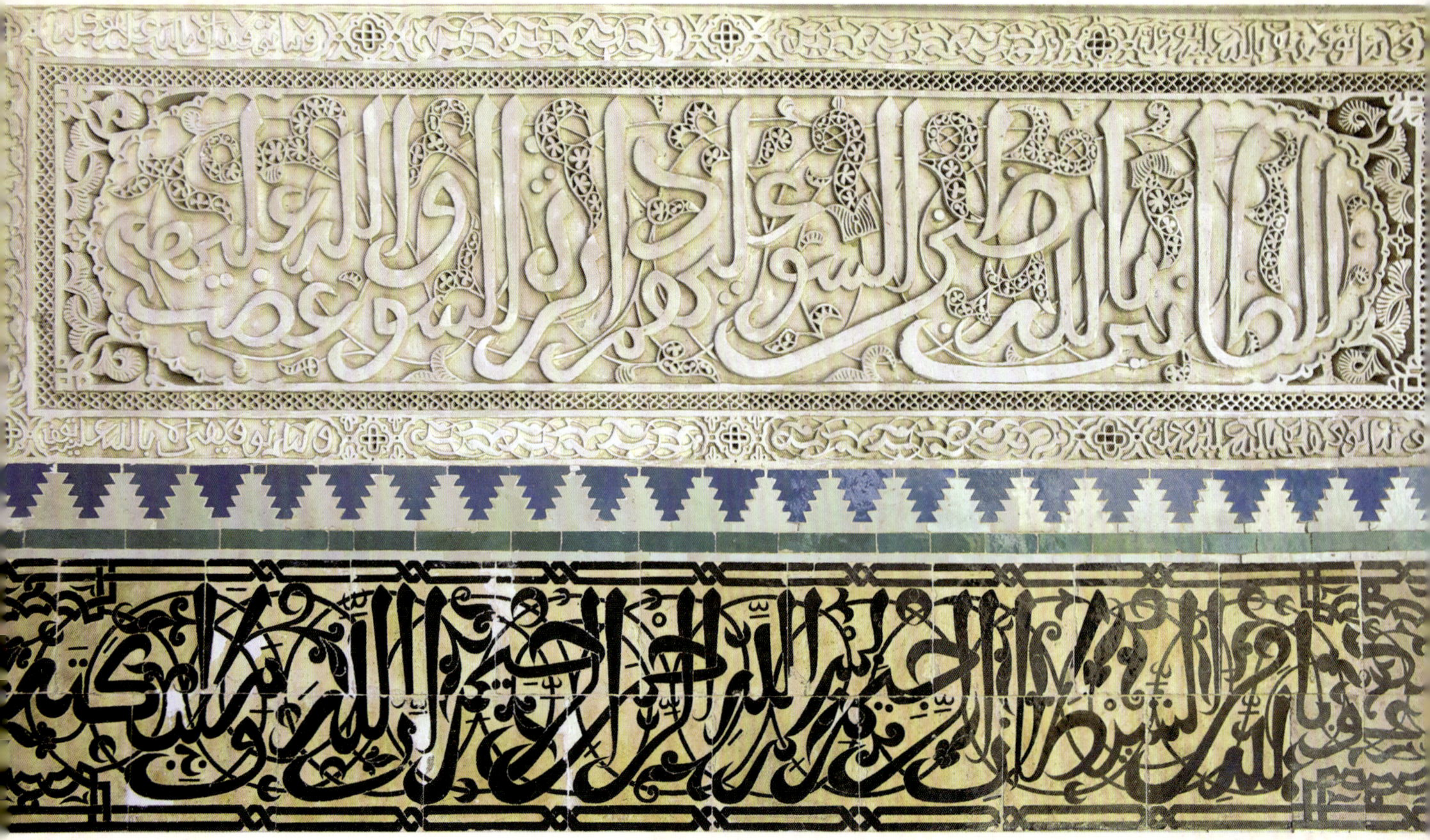

Panel from the Madrasah al-'Attārīn

If we have chosen our examples in architecture, it is due to the central role that it occupies in artistic creation since a whole series of other arts are attached to it, such as carpentry, stucco work, mosaic work, and even calligraphy which, in other respects, represents the most independent and noble of the arts, serving as it does to visually fix the divine Word. Sacred calligraphy, which attained an unprecedented perfection in the world of Islam, is as regards the Koran and its text, analogous in the visual order to psalmody of the Koran in the auditory order. This psalmody was encouraged by the Prophet himself and creates a kind of link between the revealed Word and music, just as calligraphy creates a link with the Word of the Koran and visual art. And let us take the opportunity to point out that Maghribi calligraphy, notably Moroccan calligraphy which is hardly distinguishable from its Andalusian sister, has preserved more ancient, and therefore more hieratic, characteristics as compared with most of the calligraphic styles of the East.[7]

[7] Each region, each cultural milieu, of the Islamic world, developed a certain style of writing which is immediately recognizable. However, this does not mean that this style is practiced exclusively, since it is always possible that a Moroccan calligrapher may write in the style of Egypt or Central Asia, or that he may use a form of "Kūfic" found in Samarkand. Nonetheless, there exists a typically Maghribi style common to Morocco, Andalusia, and medieval Algeria which has had an influence from as far as the Sahel to the coasts of Africa near the equator.

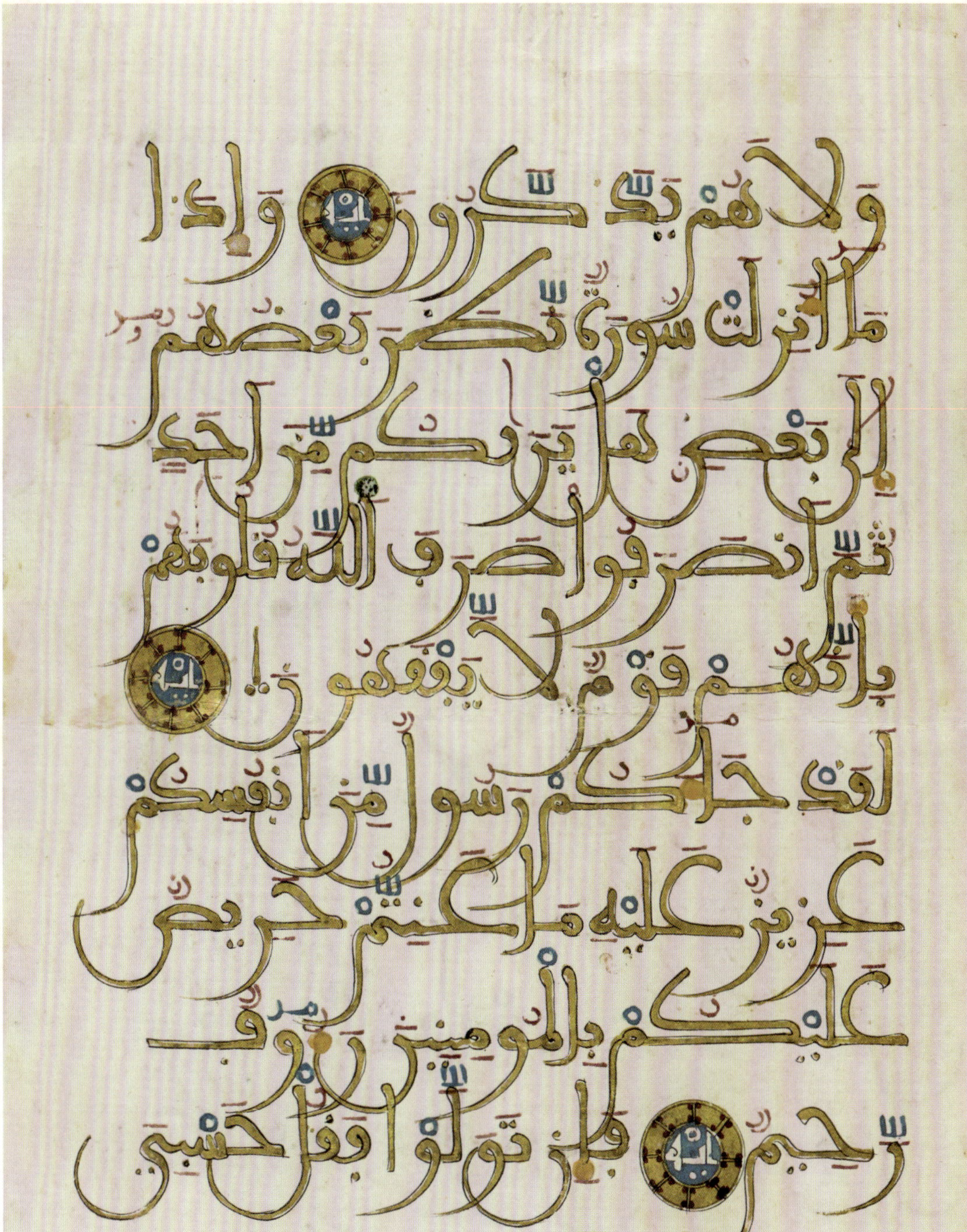

Page from a 13th century Maghribi-style Koran from Andalusia

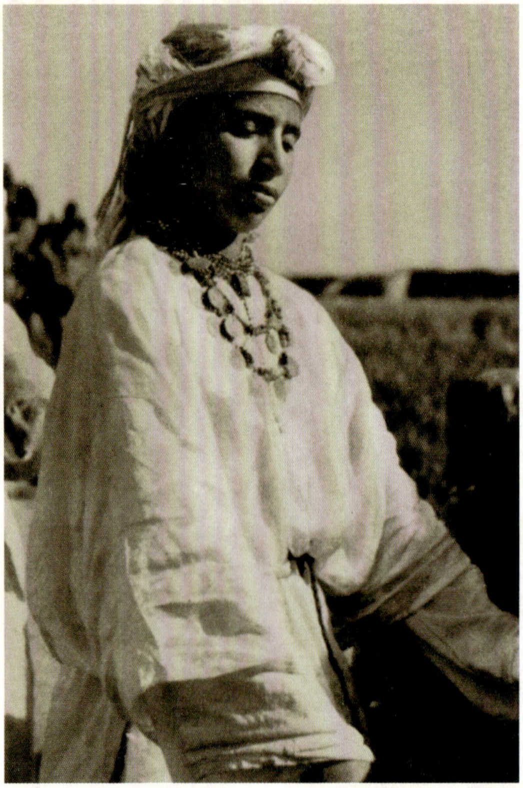

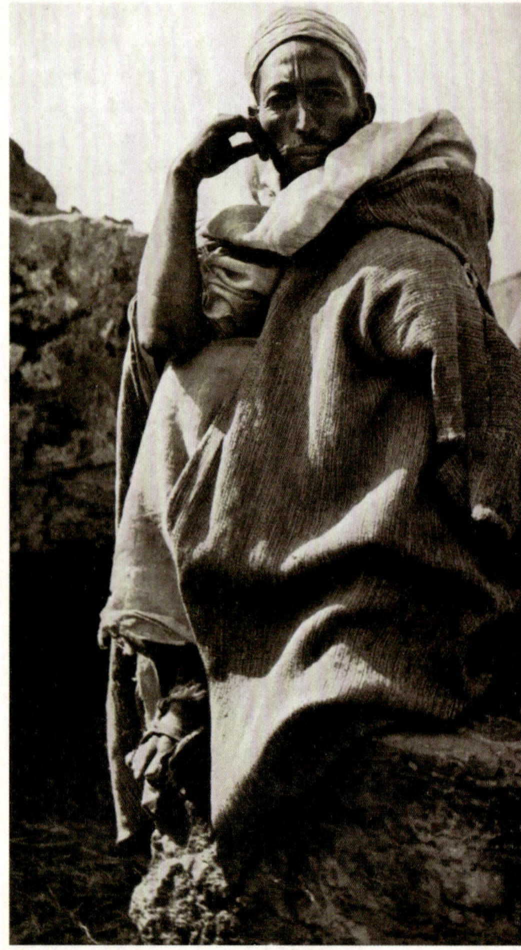

Ibn Khaldūn distinguishes between the arts attached to architecture and those independent of it. Among the latter one can distinguish first of all the various trades related to the production of furnishings in the broad sense of the term, such as the ones practiced by carpenters, coppersmiths, and potters, without forgetting carpet and mat weavers. Cloth weavers and tailors are attached to the art of dress, and one could add jewelers to that category, if their technique did not make its own category. The same is true for leather workers as well as for armorers, saddlers, and harness makers: their trades are indirectly attached to dress and to personal adornment. But there are many other categories to establish, starting with those of urban arts and Bedouin arts, a distinction which falls into the much broader sedentary-nomad polarity whose laws Ibn Khaldūn masterfully traced. There are the typically sedentary arts, of which architecture is the most important, and the typically nomadic arts, such as the art of the knotted carpet, which is the furniture *par excellence* of the Bedouin tent and is not urban except by adoption. There is also the art of Bedouin pottery as well as the arts of jewelry and leather work in the service of nomads and semi-nomads. As for metal work, it is sedentary by its technique, but is often developed in the service of nomads: one need only think of the edged weapons produced for the Bedouin.[8]

[8] All that is nomadic bears the imprint of the warlike virtues of strength of determination and nobility, qualities which have their place in the spiritual economy of Islam, so much so that one finds their traces nearly everywhere in Islamic art, including architecture.

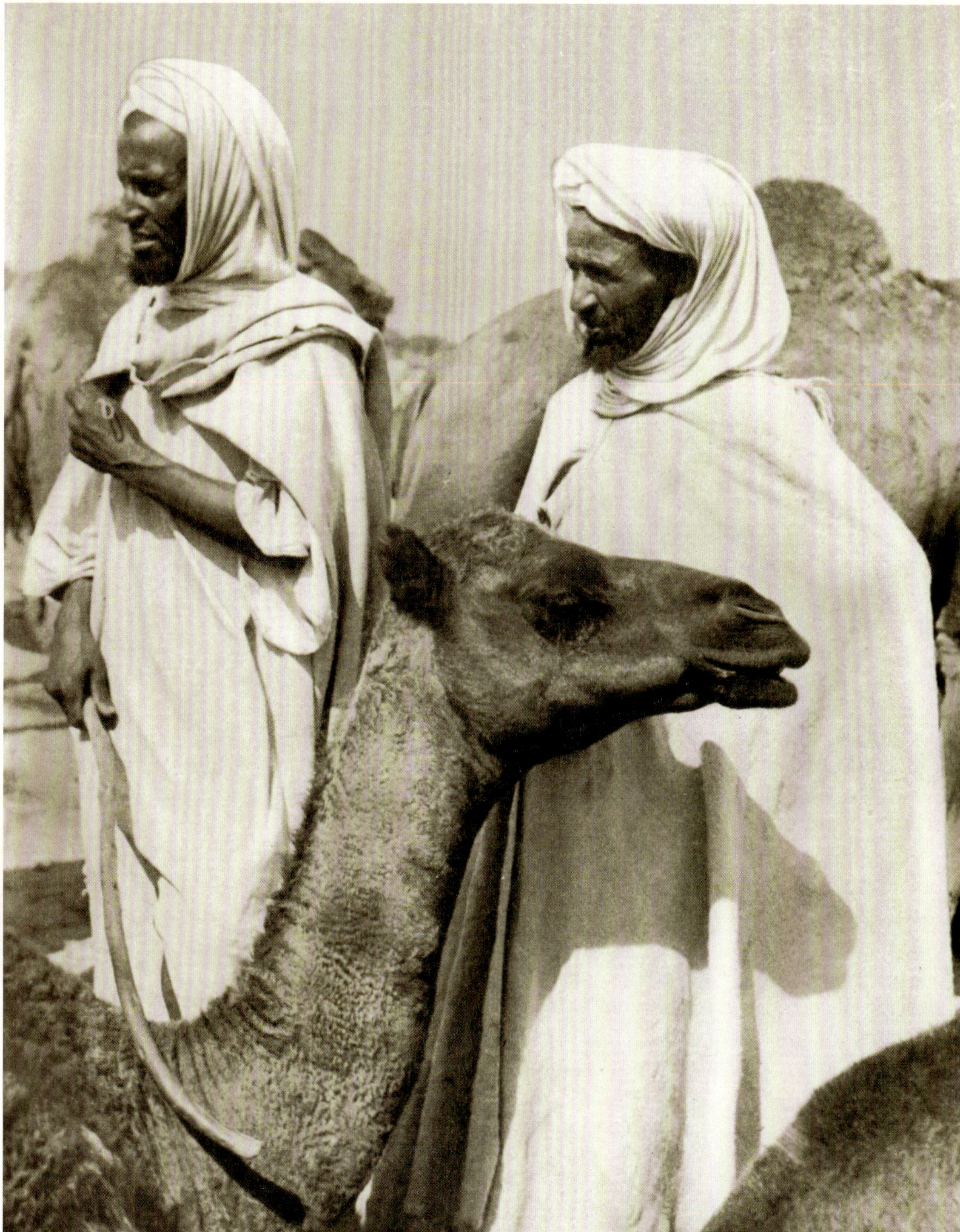

Above: Arab nomads from the Mulūya Valley; *Opposite left*: Berber bride with jewelry; *Opposite right*: Berber from the Middle Atlas

There is the sedentary element and the nomadic element, the city and the countryside, the Arabs and Berbers, and all these antagonisms, or more exactly complementarities, are combined to various degrees in Moroccan art. But let us return to architecture and examine the composition of a Maghribi mosque and its derivation. Mosque architecture developed differently in the various parts of the Islamic world, but always at the base of a mosque's plan is found the memory of the first of mosques, that of Medina, built in the time of the Prophet. This mosque consisted of a courtyard (*ṣaḥn*), onto one side of which a series of small houses or cabins for the Prophet and his family were attached. In this domestic courtyard, which measured around a hundred elbows in width and depth, a shelter was constructed along the *qiblah* wall, in the south, for those who said the prayer in the courtyard. It was covered with a roof made of branches and clay and held up by palm trunks. The courtyard thus prolonged the prayer hall when the latter could not hold all the faithful. On the opposite side of the courtyard was a smaller shelter, the famous *ṣuffah*, a sort of gallery or raised seating area where the poorest of the Prophet's companions could find shade.

The mosques of Arab countries and especially those of the Maghrib faithfully preserve this original and primitive arrangement. The palm trunks supporting the roof of the prayer hall have been replaced by pillars or columns, or even by rows of arcades, and the covering of branches has been replaced by gabled roofs. As for the *ṣuffah*, it has been transformed into galleries which surround the *ṣaḥn* and which still serve as a shelter for the poor and for travelers.

The prayer hall extends more in width than in depth, in keeping with the ordering of the faithful in lines behind the *imām*. A sort of elevated transept often indicates the position of the *miḥrāb* and the extension of its axis to the courtyard. The form of the *miḥrāb*—mark of the *qiblah*—has been attributed to a Christian origin. It is possible that the apses of the Byzantine or Coptic churches inspired Umayyad architects with the idea of giving to the *miḥrāb* the form of a niche. In any case, if there is a borrowing here it is justified by the very meaning of the term which, in the Koran, designates a place of refuge or retreat, where one can isolate oneself from the world in order to worship God. In a mosque, only the *imām* isolates himself by placing himself in the niche of the *miḥrāb*, but it is precisely he who pronounces the sacred words in the name of the community. The minaret likewise did not exist in the time of the Prophet, and its form has both pagan and Christian precedents; but no one would contest its legitimacy, which stems from its function. The same applies to the fountain usually located in the middle of the *ṣaḥn*.

All these architectural elements are already to be found in the first and still-existing Umayyad mosque, that of Damascus, and they succeeded in reaching Fez by way of Kairouan as well as Córdoba. What distinguishes Maghribi mosques, and more particularly those of Morocco and Algeria, is the great simplicity and sobriety with which they apply the aforementioned models. And in this they are models as much for the present as for the future, since what is at once true and simple is never out-of-date.

We have seen that the mosque and the Arab house both have their origin in the domestic courtyard onto which living spaces open either directly or beneath the shadow of galleries. This is an architecture turned towards the interior; from the outside it often seems bare and impoverished, when in fact its richness remains within.

The modalities and forms of architectural decoration are essentially the same, be it a case of a mosque or a house. This impersonal and

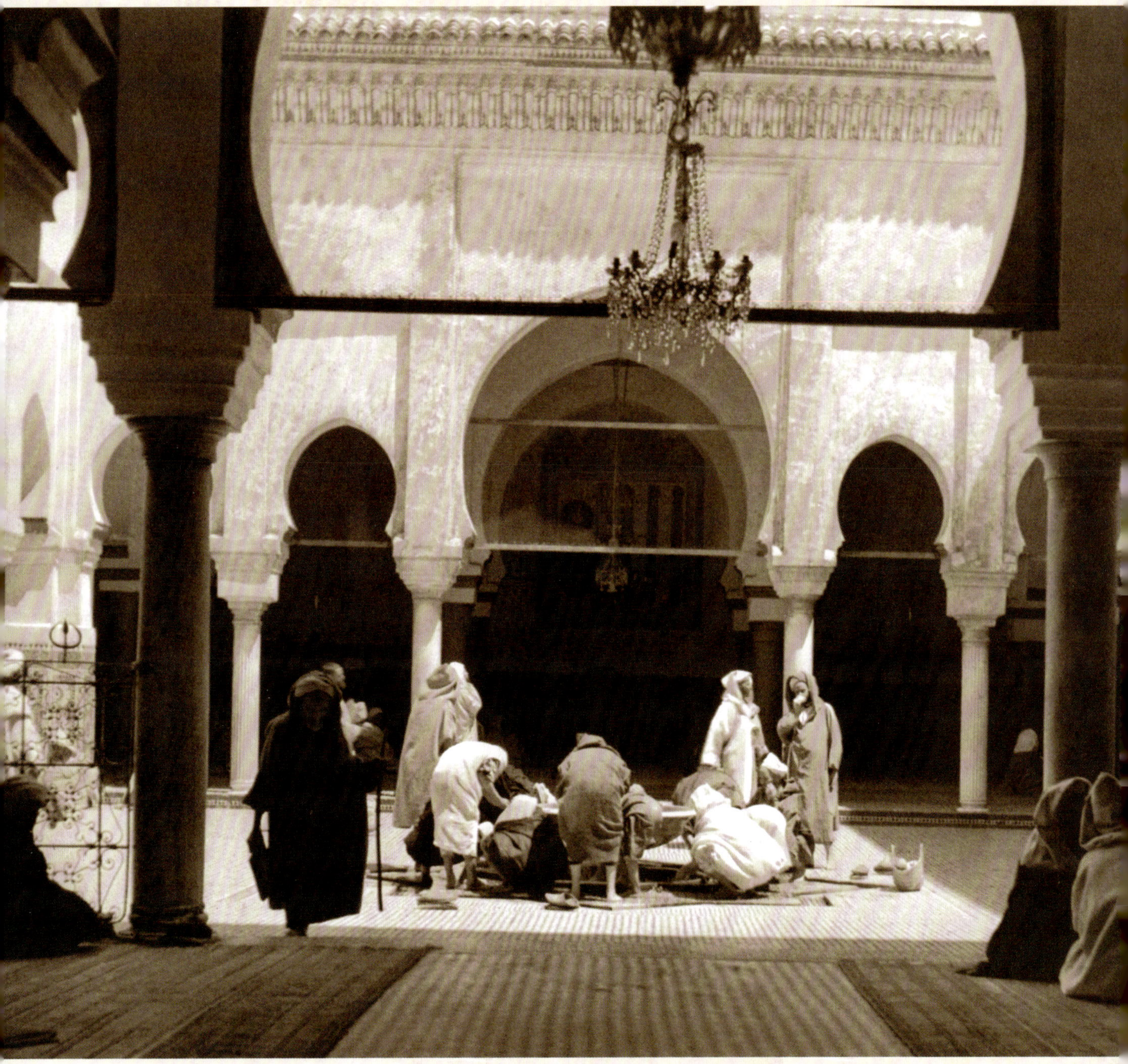

Worshippers making ritual ablutions in the inner courtyard of the Mūlay Idrīs II Mausoleum-Mosque

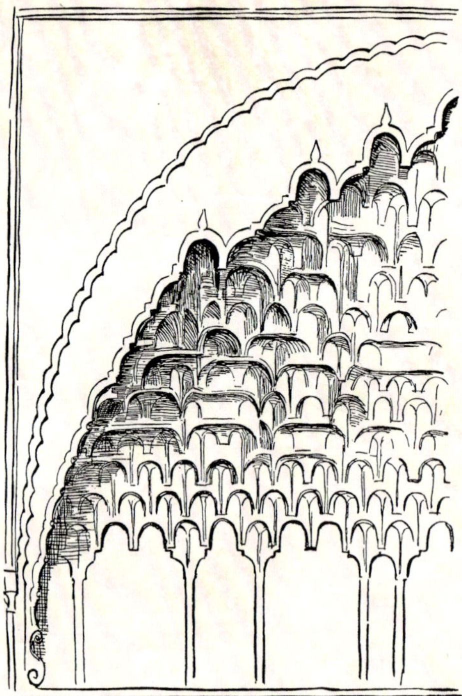

Detail of a niche with "honeycomb" ornaments of sculptured stucco

objective decoration never allows the introduction of a subjective note into the ambience of a house or a mosque. One could say that its forms result from the very nature of the material used, ceramic, plaster, and wood, as well as from the universal laws of rhythm, chromatic harmony, and geometry. Despite this impersonal character—or rather, one should say, because of this character—the ambience created by Maghribi art inspires a certain state of soul, of serenity and peace, which brings us back to the fundamental attitude of the Muslim.

Maghribi art shares these qualities with the art of all Muslim peoples, but one can affirm without exaggeration that it is in the Maghrib that Islamic art, by emptying itself of all naturalistic influences, attains to a sort of crystalline purity found nowhere else. Let us note in passing that Maghribi art, although truly an "abstract" art in that it excludes all imitation of nature, is nevertheless situated at the antipodes of the so-called "abstract art" of modern Europe—an art which is above all a reaction against the naturalism of the nineteenth century and which in no wise escapes the vicious circle of a reaction since it preserves the cult of individual subjectivity. This fact necessarily prevents it from taking on a universally valid and objective language, for the absence of artistic individualism exists only upon the foundation of a tradition. The latter reflects in its way, on the plane of forms, the love of truth and detachment, virtues which, in the Islamic context, are directly attached to *tawḥīd.*

Everything, in the art of Islam, is attached to *tawḥīd*, including in particular the rejection of illusionistic means, such as perspective in painting, which gives to a flat surface the appearance of three-dimensional space, or naturalism in sculpture, which confers on stone the semblance of a living body.[9] In Islam, each thing is put in its place: a painted surface will always be a surface and a stone always a stone; all illusion or false reality is excluded, in function of the first and fundamental distinction, that of the absolute and the relative, expressed by the testimony *lā ilāha illa 'Llāh* ("There is no divinity save God").

Love of rhythm and geometry also flows from *tawḥīd*, for rhythm is the reflection of unity in time, while regular geometric figures reflect it in space. It is here neither a question of an interpretation *a posteriori* nor of a

[9] This is why miniature art retains only the linear contours and colors of the things represented. Naturally there are exceptions in all domains, exceptions which only confirm the rule. In the Islamic world, when one finds works in cast iron or embossed metal which directly and boldly imitate animal or even human forms, one can be certain that they are either "curiosa" (*'ajā'ib*) made for some prince who is not concerned with traditional rules, or objects related to magical customs.

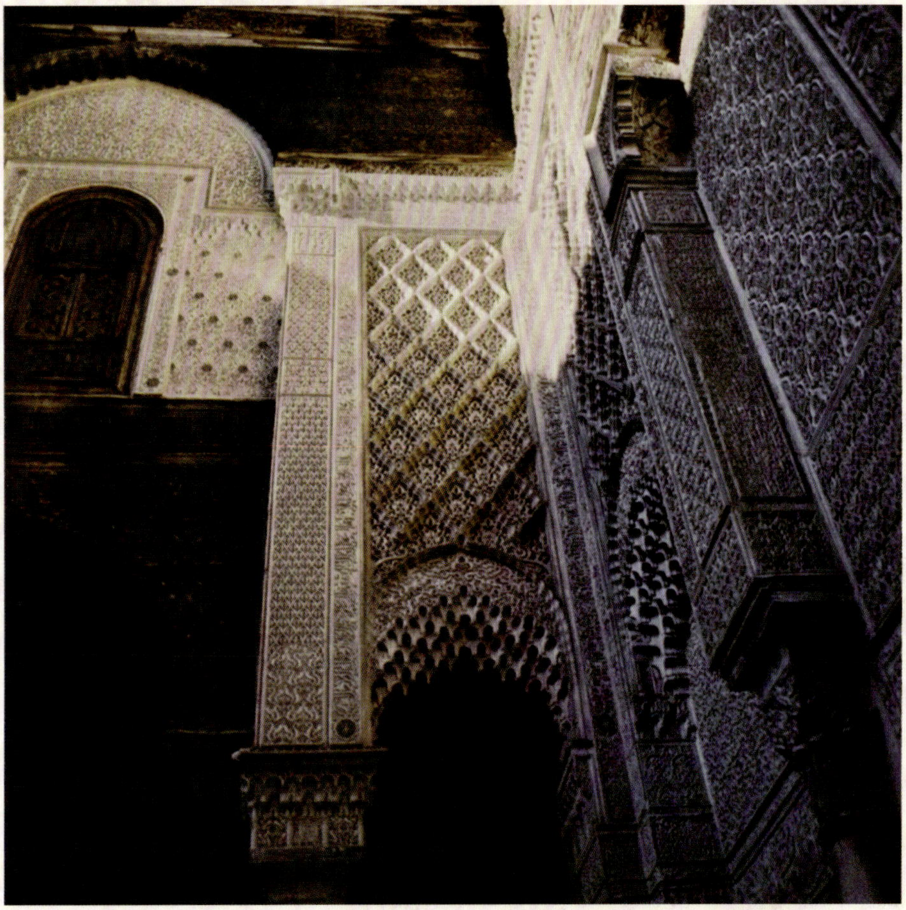

Decoration and sculptured plaster and cedar wood in Madrasah al-'Attārīn

speculation foreign to Islam, but simply of a symbolism inherent in the nature of things. The Maghribi artist is very often a contemplative who finds in the visible signs of the invisible.

The most obvious artistic symbolism of *tawḥīd* is undoubtedly that of light, a symbolism which moreover has its basis in the Koran: "God is the Light of the heavens and the earth" (24:35). Be it modified, colored, or attenuated by shadows, light always remains unique and essential light. Its nature does not change, but permits of an infinite number of gradations between brightness and darkness, and between the different colors. The true substance of Maghribi art is light: the mosaics of enameled tile reflect and refract it into colors, and the ornaments of sculptured stucco capture and distil it, the walls in both cases seeming to become translucent. As for the darker wooden panels, which constitute the special charm of Moroccan architecture, they enhance by way of contrast the luminous character of the other elements.

The inner façade of a mosque or a Moroccan house—the façade turned towards the courtyard—is as if woven of light. The latter removes from the walls all their heaviness: the body of the building becomes vibrant light, while the light, in itself intangible, is turned to crystal.

Inna 'Llāha jamīlun yuḥibbu 'l-jamāl ("Verily, God is beautiful and He loveth beauty").

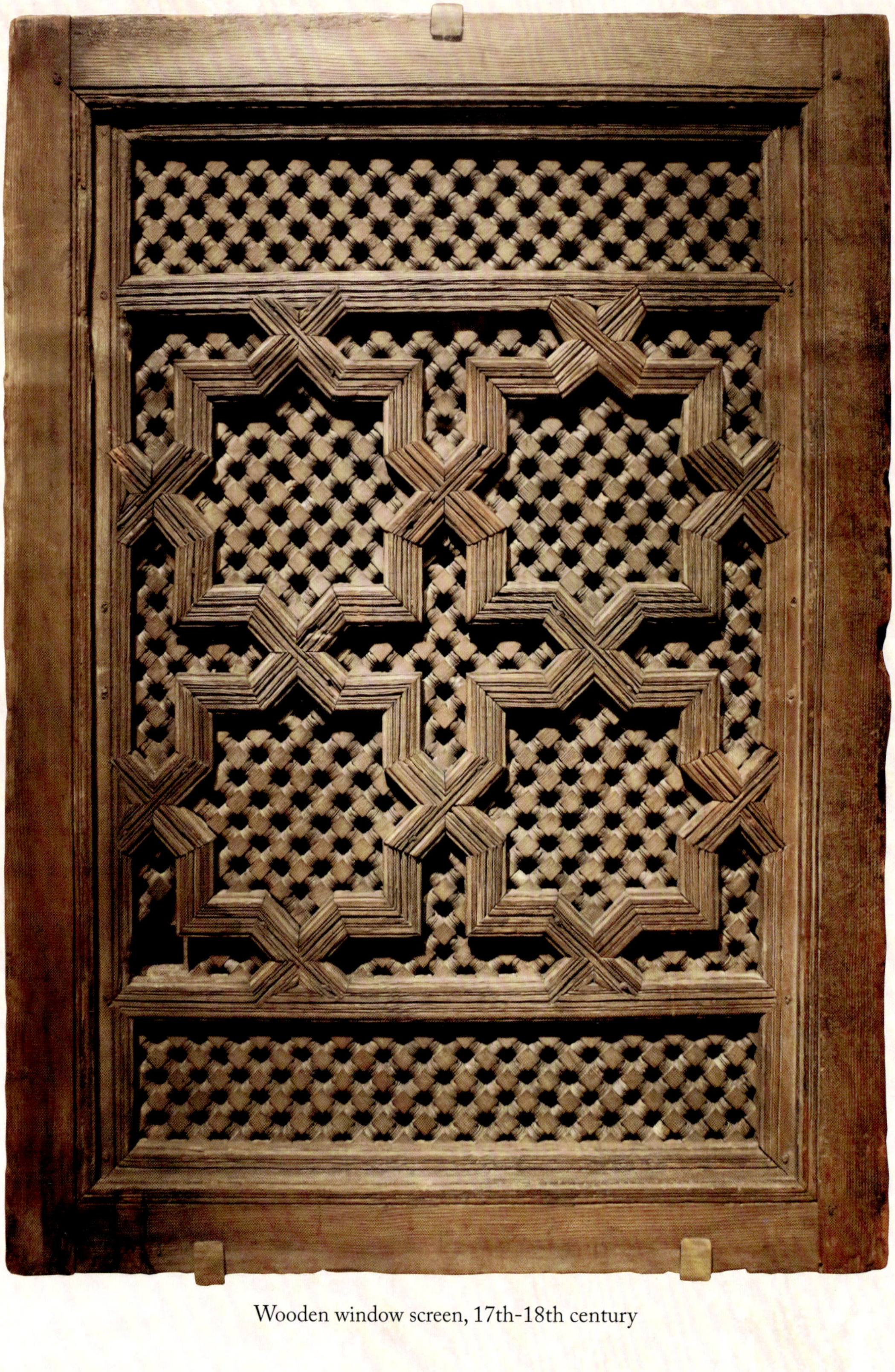

Wooden window screen, 17th-18th century

Chapter 4

Traditional Craftsmanship: Its Nature and Destiny

How to define the role of the craftsman? Should one distinguish, on the one hand, between the role of the artist who creates freely and, on the other hand, that of the worker who fashions things with a purely utilitarian objective? But the distinction between the artist and the craftsman is an ambiguous one, which classical Arabic, moreover, does not make: *ṣāniʿ* is equally the artist and the craftsman, and this is highly significant. Traditionally, the artist or craftsman is the man who fashions an object in view of its perfection, which implies not only its usefulness but also its beauty, for according to the *ḥadīth*: "God has prescribed excellence (= beauty) for all things" (*Inna 'Llāha kataba 'l-iḥsāna ʿalā kulli shay*). The artist in this framework is always a craftsman in that his shaping of objects never represents "art for art's sake" but responds to a practical need; and the craftsman is an artist to the extent that he aspires to the perfection of his work.

The scission between art and craftsmanship is a relatively recent phenomenon of strictly European origin. Its corollary is the scission between the craftsman who creates beautiful objects, and the worker who produces objects with a purely utilitarian purpose, objects which may be beautiful or ugly according to the case, but which most often are ugly, even and above all when some entirely artificial decoration is added to the object bearing no relation to its nature. It is modern European civilization that has invented the ugliness of objects for everyday use. This must be stated given the truth that traditional civilizations, like that of old Morocco, never knew truly ugly objects: a cup, a piece of cloth, a chest could be very simple, even rudimentary, without ever being ugly, as one can still easily observe in the countryside and in Moroccan villages;[1] and this absence of ugliness or this almost natural beauty is a badge of glory belonging to the most humble of traditional trades.

The craftsman or artist creates by means of a tool which in effect is but the extension of his hand, whose mark the fashioned object will always bear. The tool—a weaving loom for example—can impose upon the artist a relative monotony, but it will never impose upon him an absolute uniformity, which corresponds to the machine alone. Everything produced by machine is characterized by a perfect repetition which seems to contradict the very laws of life. It is true that nature herself ceaselessly reproduces the same vegetable and animal forms and that the craftsman too merely repeats certain transmitted models, but this repetition is never mathematical and quasi-absolute as in the case of machine-made productions.

The search for beauty, moreover, obliges the craftsman to begin again, always from the ground up. Each of his works will be a new trial, and that is why each of them bears something inimitable and personal; its small irregularities confer on it the charm of some-

[1] Modern ugliness, sadly, is now rapidly encroaching into small Moroccan towns and even the countryside. —Editors' Note

thing living and not dead, whereas the perfect repetition which characterizes machine-made products kills the very perfume of life. When, for example, Bedouin carpet weavers are assembled into collective workshops where they follow carefully calculated designs, this charm is naturally lost and is hardly replaced by modern "artistic creations," which no longer have any vital link to the fundamental forms of this art. When quantity dominates production, quality is killed—this is an inexorable law.

We said that the hands of the craftsman confer upon each of his works something unique. However, one must not believe that the craftsman or artist—he is both at the same time—proceeds by an arbitrary or individualistic choice of forms. The formal language of the arts is faithful to the spirit of Islam, which excludes subjectivism and promethean fantasies. For the artist, it is a question not of feeling, but of method: tradition has put at his disposal an ensemble of formal elements which constitute a language and which must be used according to the laws inherent to this language, such that one could speak of a grammar or syntax of forms which one can master but not violate. The forms themselves, however, can and should be developed according to circumstances, in a manner analogous to the development of a "mode" in traditional music, where there is a certain sonorous scale, then modes, and finally melodic schemes which can be developed on the outline of a given mode. This law, though strict, guarantees at the same time a certain creative liberty, for, thanks to it, traditional musicians can improvise on the impulse of the moment without ever being in dissonance with their orchestra companions.

The example of music—we are thinking of the music called "Andalusian"—can be transposed without difficulty to the visual arts,

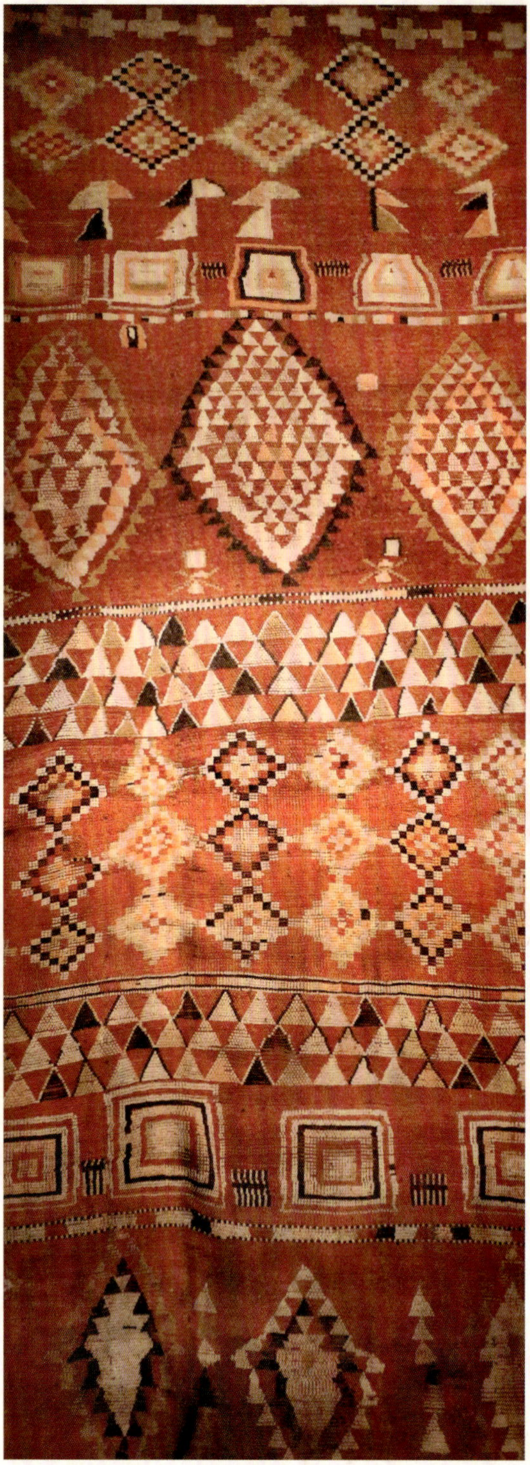

Above: Berber rug from Ahmar, c. 1900-1920;
Opposite: Mosaic work from Fez, 14th-16th century

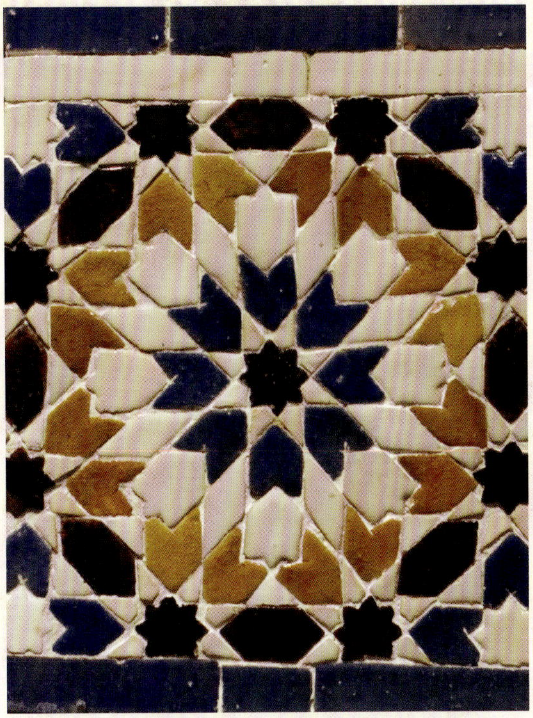

such as the mosaic work of enameled faience. A master of this art of *zillīj* has at his disposal a certain range of colors—dark blue, mars violet, red, brown, ocher, almond green, and milky white—that is determined by the minerals naturally available and traditionally used for this purpose. And he knows a certain number of shapes into which he will cut the pieces, each shape having its name and role in the geometric development of the mosaic. These few elements suffice for him to compose an almost unlimited variety of ornaments, and in particular the geometric rosettes which interpenetrate and interlace in perfect continuity.

A first rule of art—a rule which should be self-evident, but which too many craftsmen seem nowadays to forget—requires that an object's form—its general form as well as its decoration—correspond to a purpose. A vase, for example, is made to contain liquid, hence its relatively ample belly and its narrower neck, made to direct the poured contents. A vase whose sides are perforated like a basket or pigeon cage is neither a vessel nor a lamp, but a sort of bastard object evoking, perhaps, a feeling of the unexpected but also of the equivocal. The same applies to certain fashionable vases made of terracotta and covered with pressed and partially gilded leather: this facing is neither suited to the object's purpose—the leather makes the vase no more watertight—nor needed for its embellishment; in short, it gives only the impression of a strange and artificial luxury.[2] Love of the artificial for the sake of the artificial is nothing other than poor taste. An artist's work consists of conferring upon each thing the perfection potentially contained in its own nature, like the crystal that is potentially contained in the raw mineral. In its state of perfection, "each thing praises its creator," and this creator is not the artist, but God.

A second rule, no less important, holds that a work's aesthetic effect should be obtained with a minimum of elements. To waste an entire arsenal of means to achieve a merely mediocre effect is certainly not art. This principle of economy of means in no wise forbids the occasional display of the "peacock's tail," but it does condemn whatever adds nothing to a work's beauty and which, by this very fact, harms its essential expression. The Moroccan artists who decorated the inner façades of the *madāris* with an incredible richness of detail did not forget the principle of economy, and they knew how to alternate preciously ornamented walls with perfectly empty surfaces. They made the richness even more precious by the presence of a certain poverty, and they ennobled the poverty by the beauty.

[2] This was a popular craft innovation of the 1960s and '70s. These and other such "bastard" objects abound on the Moroccan handicraft market today. —Editors' Note

The normal place for the craftsman is in the souk. The grouping of the trades by streets or quarters corresponds to the existence of professional guilds, which are now tending to disintegrate because their customary laws, highly efficacious in the craft environment and full of moral teachings, have been replaced by the more indirect regulations of modern administration. Everyone regrets this change without being able to remedy it. First to disappear was the authority of the *amīn*, the "man of trust" chosen by each guild whose judgment was definitive in the case of a dispute between members of the same guild; the pasha or governor of the city consulted him, and then settled the matter according to the latter's view. The *amīn* was elected from among the masters of the trade. He had to enjoy unblemished professional and moral repute,[3] and he also had to have an in-depth knowledge of customary law, the *'urf*, though he received no salary for his expertise. The various *'umanā'* (plural of *amīn*) were subordinate to the *muḥtasib*, who controlled the quality of goods and their prices.

This professional organization goes back to the Middle Ages and was generally common to all Muslim cities. As a collective foundation for work, it realizes in its way an ideal which modern sociologists have sought in vain to attain by other means: the equilibrium between individual liberty and collective solidarity, with its guarantees of security and order. It is sometimes argued that this corporative organization suffocates creativity by preventing free competition. In actual fact, each craftsman competes with the others by the quality of his own product; and he is also free in the sense that he is his own supervisor who can work as and when he wants. On the other hand, dishonest competition on the basis of poor-quality materials is effectively excluded, as each is obliged to observe certain rules embodied in the code of professional honor (*'urf*). While it is inevitable that the trades will change, let us nonetheless hope that the wise principles of the old order will be maintained.

In this context it is appropriate to say a few words about commerce which is typical, not only of Fez, but of every Muslim town that has kept its traditional structure. A small linguistic example will help us to put things in their place. We are thinking of the change in meaning undergone by the Arabic term *rizq* as it passed into the commercial jargon of Italian and French merchants of the Renaissance. The English word "risk," the French *risque*, and the Italian *rischio* are all derived from the Arabic *rizq* which means, not a possible loss, as in its English, French, and Italian homologues, but, quite the opposite, a possible gain or, more precisely, what falls to every living being by way of subsistence. Whence this inversion of meaning? For the European merchant, profit is the result of a commercial transaction, foreseeable in principle; risk is the unforeseen. For the Arab and Muslim merchant, profit, on the contrary, is unforeseeable, even though predestined, whereas the commercial transaction is but an occasional cause (*sabab*), a net cast in the hope that gain, or predestined sustenance, will manifest itself. Thus the margin of "unforeseens" does not have the same significance for the one as for the other: for the European merchant it is negative, for the Arab or Muslim, positive. In terms of accounting, their respective modes of operation are no different but their attitudes are divergent and hence also their customs. It is from this perspective that the role of auction sales, so frequent in the medina, must be seen, as well as the habit of bargaining: prices are fluid, the opportunities for unforeseen profit are increased.

[3] The term *amīn* points to the *sunnah*, from which this institution derived. As is well known, the name *amīn* was given by the Arabs of Mecca to Muhammad before he received his prophetic mission.

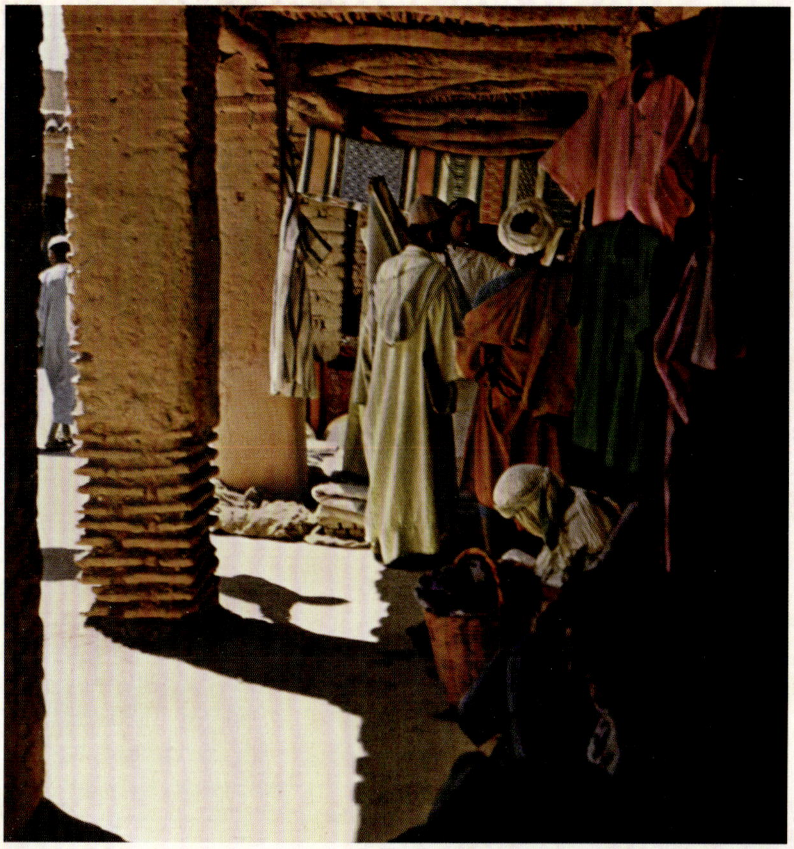

Left: Cloth and clothing market in the South. Next to the hand-woven carpets are cheap products of modern industry;
Bottom: Merchants in the grain market

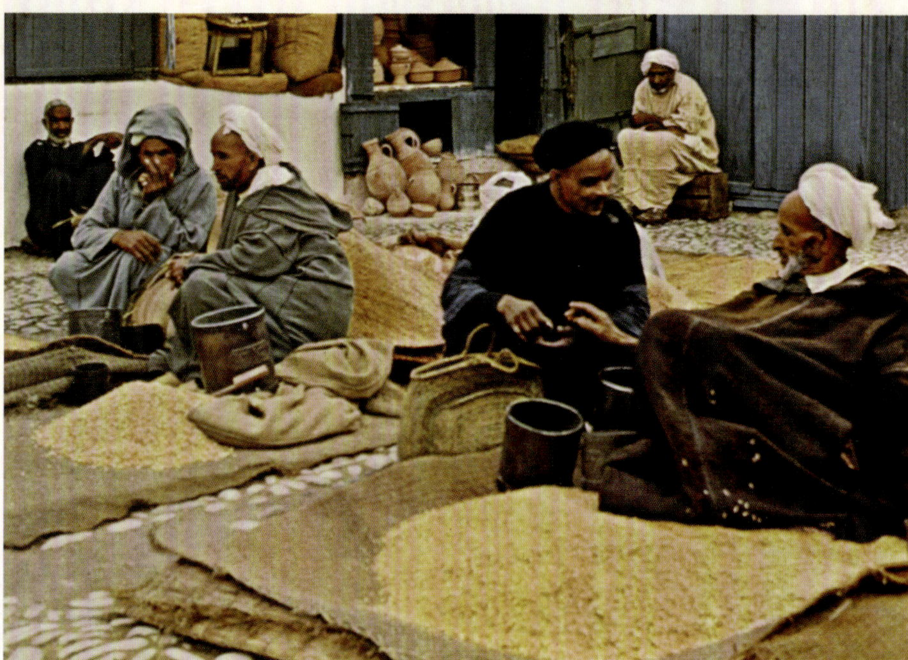

Let us also point out that, despite everything, one reason the crafts continue to prosper is because they form a part of a whole system of economics wherein the money invested is minimal and the material lost is practically nil. Materials such as skins, wool, or silk arrive at the town in a raw state and undergo a series of transformations passing from one skilled hand to another until there is nothing left to waste; even cows' horns and oil-cake from the olive presses are used as working materials. The craftsman needs no capital, for he often buys his materials on credit, and his instruments are of the simplest sort. His entire trade lies in his expertise, whereas industry is based on the machine, which is an instrument that has become more or less autonomous to the point where it determines the work's rhythm and even the object's style.

This leads us to consider the present situation of the Moroccan crafts and their chances of survival. According to a widespread opinion, these crafts are doomed to gradually disappear in favor of industry, for in the long term, it is thought, manual labor will be unable to resist competition from the machine. It is believed that this change is generally good, since it should go along with an overall increase in the material standard of living. One can only hope that the transition from hand-made production to machine-made production will take place without too much social upheaval, while wishing in particular that a certain qualitative craftsmanship, now referred to by the pleonasm of "artistic craftsmanship" (*artisanat d'art*), can survive in a semi-industrialized form in order to satisfy the needs of tourism and export. This way of viewing things seems to be perfectly realistic, yet is not, since it overlooks the fact that craftsmanship corresponds to a human need which industry could never satisfy.

The opinion that craftsmanship should disappear is founded upon the apparently undeniable statistics according to which the more a country is "developed" in terms of its "standard" of living, the more its industry will be developed and its craftsmanship reduced. These statistics, like all one-sided arguments, ignore two things: firstly, that a good can be accompanied by an evil and that, beyond a certain point, this evil will be greater than the good; secondly, that the more a movement accelerates, the faster it arrives at its turning point: what was scorned yesterday will be sought after tomorrow, by the very fact that it has become rare.

Let us consider the evil that accompanies industrial development and let us note right

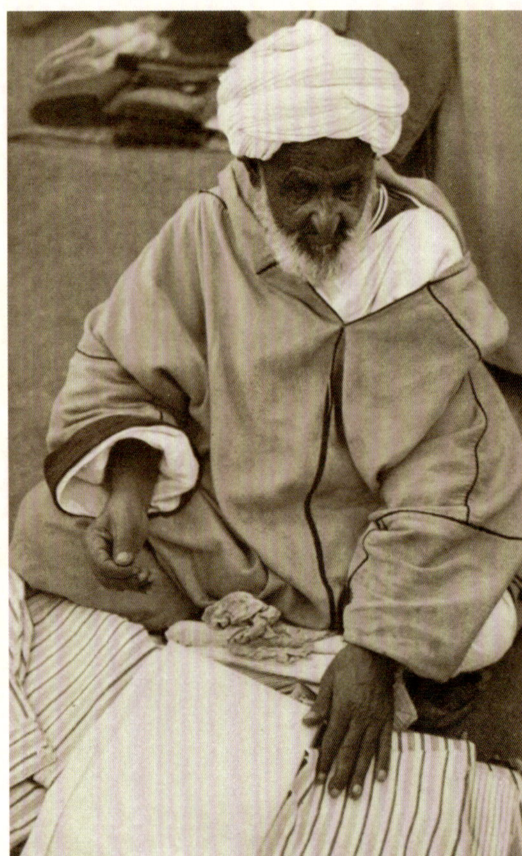

Merchant in the cloth market

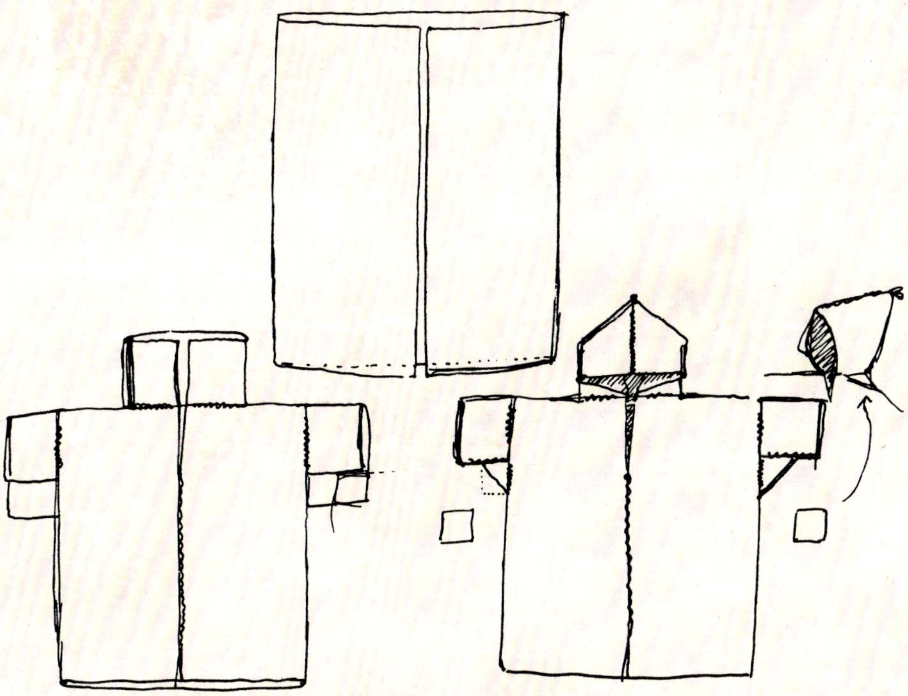

Pattern for a traditional robe (*jalābah*)

away that it is in those countries where the benefits of industry seem most obvious that the negative side of industry is most strongly felt. One need only visit the large industrial centers of Europe to notice that the relative well-being of the toiling masses hides a terrible misery of soul. While the craftsman practices his trade with a certain pleasure, because it calls upon his intelligence, his imagination, and his manual skill, in short upon all of his creative faculties, the industrial worker is generally indifferent towards his work, the meaning of which he often does not even comprehend. The craftsman's hand, equipped with a very simple tool, is like the extension of his intelligence, whereas the motions of the industrial worker are dictated by the machine which he governs only in appearance, being himself in reality but a part thereof. There is no creative liberty in the industrial worker's labor, and without this liberty neither can he take any joy in it.

These considerations also help us to establish the criterion for determining whether the introduction of certain mechanical tools will, or will not, destroy the authenticity of a traditional art, namely: that whatever gives an object its form should be reserved to manual labor. Thus, for example, one can accept that a wood carver cut his cedar planks with a mechanical saw, but not that he carve their ornaments with a drill. Or again, in the art of carpet weaving, it is relatively indifferent whether a certain color is acquired by a chemical dye or a vegetable dye, provided that it has the desired tone and stability, and notwithstanding the quite special charm residing in the slight variation of intensity characteristic of vegetable dyes.[4] Finally, to give one more example,

[4] The restricted range of the old vegetable colors previously encouraged minds to the most admirable artistic innovations, while the sudden existence of a multitude of new means of expression has only brought about a temptation to adopt the easiest and most superficial solutions.

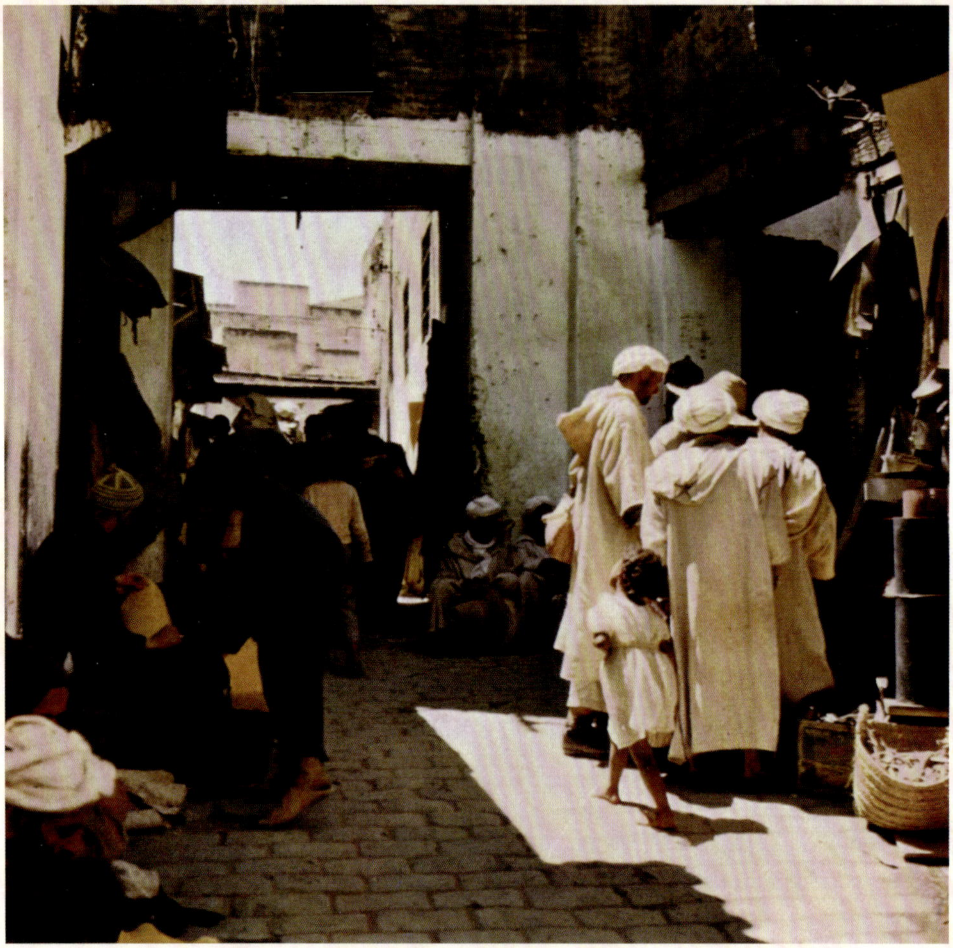

Leather market

we shall mention the case of the potter who utilizes, without prejudice to his work, an oven of modern construction. Let us note, however, that one mechanical innovation always risks inviting another, thus dragging the craftsman into the vicious circle of an ever increasing, and in the end fatal, modernization.

In an environment where almost all aspects of life are determined by industry or, more precisely, by the machine, it is no surprise that human instinct begins to react against what had hitherto been seen as pure progress, and that nostalgia for a more directly human work arises. Improvising craftsmen set up their workshops in the middle of industrial areas, merchants of hand-made objects find their customers in the most "developed" cities, and colleges and universities integrate courses in craftsmanship into their curriculum; in short, a sort of return to craftsmanship is beginning in many countries of the West. This return is very often made too late, when the authentic craft tradition, with its skill and its unity of style, has already been lost. In this respect, the Moroccan crafts possess an immense advantage, and one can rightly ask whether the expansion of industry in foreign countries, far from proving the anachronism of the Moroccan crafts, might not turn in their favor. Simply by representing the extremely rare case of a professional tradition that is still alive and in possession of its skill and its formal homogeneity, the Moroccan crafts acquire an ever greater value. However this situation may develop, there is an opportunity here that ought not to be missed: Morocco must have the courage to maintain its crafts—or shall we say, its traditional arts—against wind and tide; the day will certainly come when it will harvest the fruits of its fidelity.[5]

We are discussing fidelity because a craftsmanship whose traditional values are adulterated and corrupted by a hasty and ignorant commercialization will have no chance of survival. One expects Moroccan crafts to be typically Moroccan, and that means being rooted in their Maghribi tradition. Craftsmanship cannot really subsist unless its roots are sunk into the soil that produced it. Moroccan art or craftsmanship will live as long as its language is still understood in its own country; it is thus on Moroccans themselves that this sort of art depends, on the awareness they have of the values inherited from father to son through numerous generations, all of whom drank from the same source.

It must be said that tourism has greatly contributed to the preservation of the traditional crafts and is responsible, in particular, for the spread of hand-made products in overseas markets. However, it would be an error to believe that the survival of Moroccan art depends entirely on tourism. The latter represents an opportunity at the same time as it carries a danger, inasmuch as it encourages all sorts of compromises, from the adaptation of

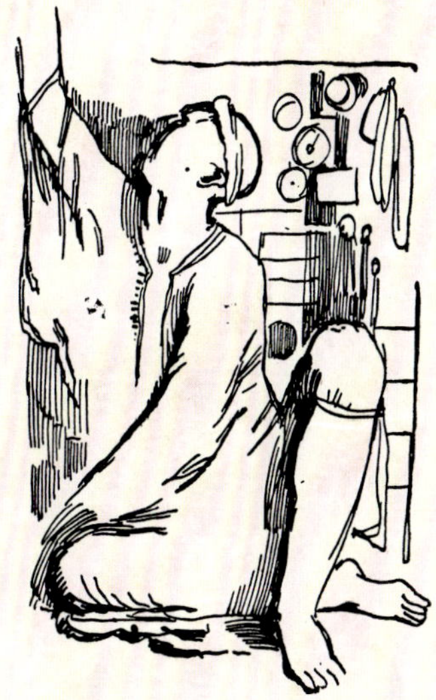

objects to the average European living room to the adulteration of style in favor of a certain shoddy exoticism. The great majority of tourists lack criteria; they want to have Moroccan art, but they are simultaneously seeking to assimilate familiar forms. There is a world of difference between a true Rabat carpet, with clear colors and geometric designs, and a carpet in Louis XIV style, yet there is no lack of "bastards" born of this double origin.

The least threatened of the craft trades are those attached to architecture and, because of this fact, they are not suited for export, other than in the case where master craftsmen are called upon to decorate a building in a foreign country.[6] Now, an "export" of this sort cannot but have a beneficial influence on the Moroccan crafts. Let us remark in passing that in Morocco the life of the two trades just mentioned largely depends on commissions from wealthy landlords and the royal court. The same craftsmen are indispensable for the restoration of historic monuments, which is yet another reason to protect these monuments.

[5] There is a project underway for a school of traditional arts in Fez which would offer general instruction on Maghribi art as well as apprenticeships in various trades. It is our hope that this school allow foreign students to take part in these internships, as there need be no fear that they would compete with Moroccan craftsmen; on the contrary, these interns should actively expand the interest in Moroccan art.

[6] This has happened many times: the great mosque of Dakar, for example, was entirely ornamented by Moroccan masters specialized in the art of tile mosaic work (*zillīj*) and of sculptured stucco work (*jibs*).

To conclude, let us observe a Muslim artist at work—a master *zillayji* who is ornamenting the walls of a mosque or a house. The construction foreman or building owner indicates the surface which the mosaic must cover and chooses the decorative motif: one or several geometrical rosettes whose lines emanate from a starred polygon and interlace in such a way as to form a continuous network, where each line radiates from a center and ends by returning to it. This motif is called "God's spider web," in remembrance of the miracle of the cave where the Prophet took refuge during his flight from Mecca to Medina: when his Meccan persecutors arrived at the cave's entrance, they saw that a spider had woven its web there and concluded that no one had yet gone through.

In the blink of an eye, the master has measured the surface and determined the number of rosettes to place onto it, as well as their geometrical model. He then begins to assemble the mosaic pieces by placing them upside down on the floor. Almost without looking, he continues his work, knowing well what sequence of geometrical elements will allow him to "link the ends" of his composition. He proceeds in this respect like the traditional musician, who "weaves" his melody on the basis of a particular "mode" prescribing certain intervals and excluding others. He has at his disposal a limited number of colors, just as the musician has at his disposal a certain scale; and the mosaic's geometrical weft is for him like unto the music's rhythm. Thus the master mosaicist, like the musician, improvises or "creates" without ever losing contact with the tradition.

"When a piece of European music begins," a master musician of the Punjab once told us, "we never know where it will end, whereas we already know that we will return to the center from which we left." This is equally true for our mosaicist: after assembling the small ceramic pieces and setting them with a layer of mortar, and after delicately detaching this mosaic sheet from the floor and applying it to the wall, we will see that the least element of his "spider web" is integrated into a harmonious ensemble, where everything radiates from a center and returns to it, in accordance with the Koranic assertion that "unto God all things are returned" (3:109).

Opposite: Tile work from the Alhambra, Granada, Spain

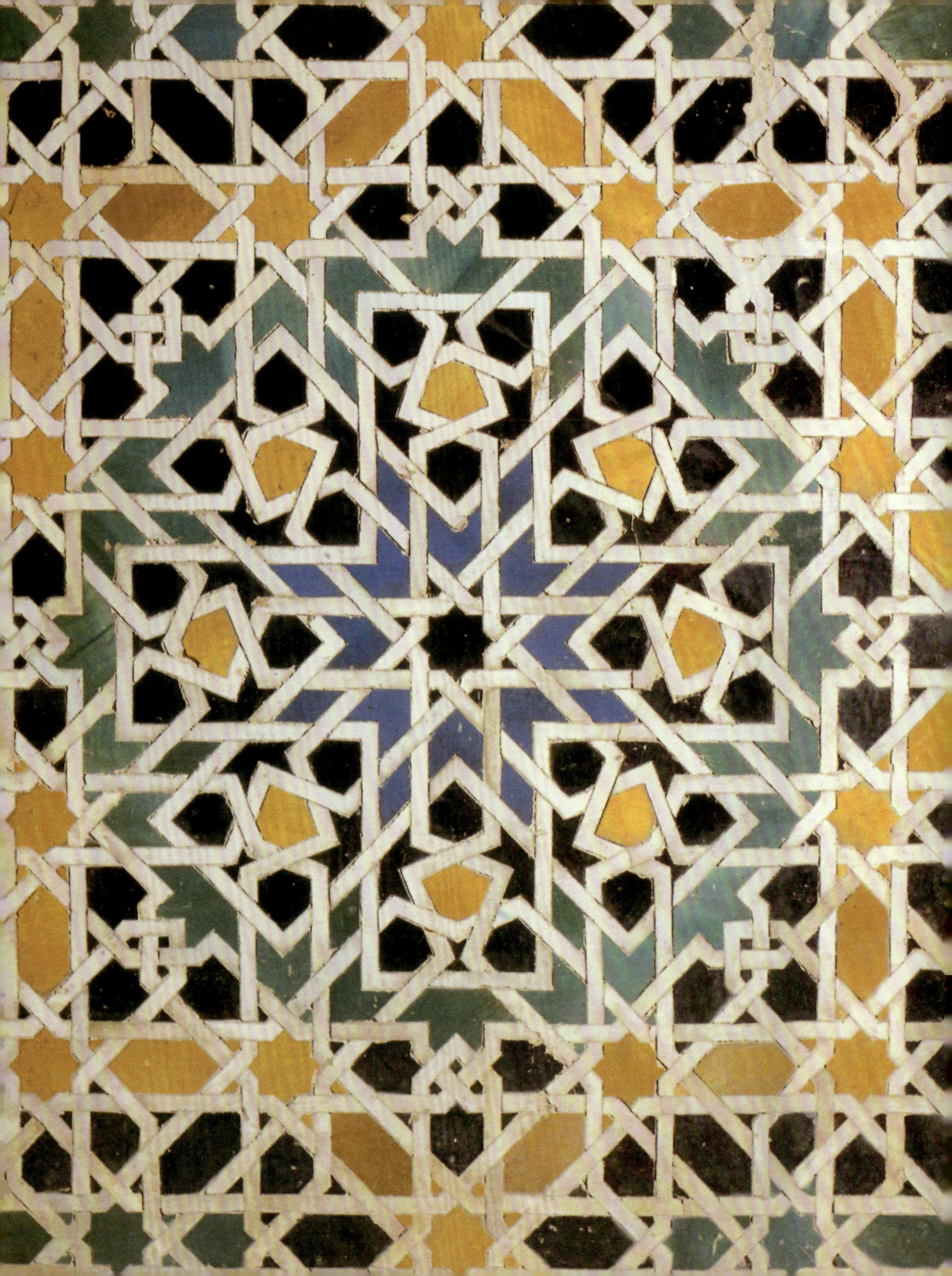

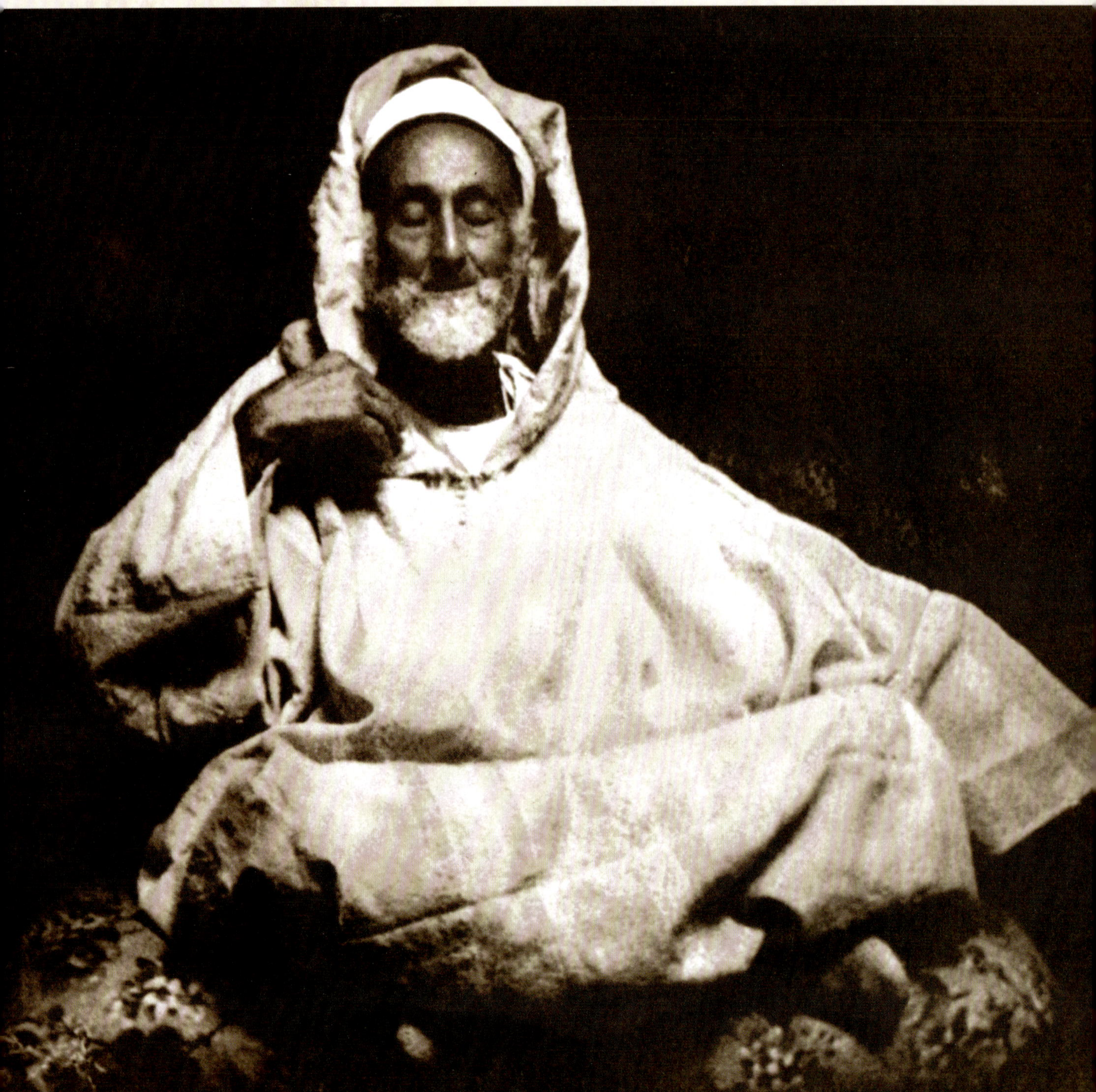

Shaykh Mūlay ʿAlī ad-Darqāwī

Appendix I

Sanctuaries of the Medina

The term "sanctuary" here covers several categories of religious buildings, whose various functions sometimes overlap with one another. The mosque (*masjid* or *jāmi'*), which is the place of prescribed and communal worship, is distinguished in principle from the *zāwiyah*, which is essentially the center of a contemplative order, and as such preserves a more or less exclusive character; nevertheless, it sometimes happens that a *zāwiyah* is used for communal worship. The mausoleum (*qabr* or *ḍarīḥ*) represents *a priori* a building set apart; nonetheless, it is never deprived of a prayer hall and it often makes up the very heart of a *zāwiyah*, the latter normally being built around the tomb of an order's founder or of a direct successor of this founder. Moreover, there are mausoleums housing the tombs of close descendants of the Prophet which are also called *zawāyā* by extension of the term and in virtue of the close connection—typical of Maghribi piety—between the chains of spiritual masters and lines of Sharīfian families. The mausoleum of the city's founding saint, Mūlay Idrīs II, is thus called a *zāwiyah* without its being attached to a particular contemplative order. In fact, it is both a funerary monument and a cathedral mosque. A fourth category of religious buildings is formed by the traditional colleges or *madāris*, which always contain a prayer hall or, more exactly, they combine student rooms with at least a teaching hall, which at the same time serves as a prayer hall.

The tendency to build great architectural complexes dedicated to several religious and social functions is not as evident in Fez as it is in the Muslim East. Nonetheless, the tendency exists and is expressed above all by the fact that the *madāris* are always attached to one or another of the great cathedral mosques: thus the *madāris* al-'Attārīn, al-Misbāhiyyāh, al-Sharrātīn, and al-Saffārīn are grouped around the great Qarawiyīn Mosque and form part of the ancient university, while the *madāris* al-Ṣahrīj and Sbāyīn are attached to the great al-'Andalūs Mosque. In the case of Bāb al-Jīssah, the mosque and college are adjoining. It is in Fās al-Jādīd, with the great mosque of Mūlay 'Abdullāh, that one finds an architectural complex analogous to the Eastern *kulliyāt*, combining a mosque with a college and a royal mausoleum.

The relationship between worship and teaching is evident at every level: many mosques house a *kursi'l-'ilm*, a teaching chair, whose costs are covered by a pious foundation (*ḥubs*), and one would be hard put to find a neighborhood mosque in Fez that does not have a Koranic school (*msīd*). Other public buildings such as the bath houses (*ḥammāmāt*, plural of *ḥammām*) are more or less directly attached to the mosques.

In a general way, this connection of various buildings expresses the fact that there is no scission in Islam between the religious order and the social order: the town's spiritual structure, insofar as it is manifested in architecture, goes hand in hand with its social structure. The spiritual structure thus reveals certain constants of urban life, even if the various communities attached specifically to this or that sanctuary do not all possess the coherence they once had. It nonetheless remains true that urban solidarity is most directly reflected in religious architecture; it is by frequenting a mosque, for example, that newly immigrated inhabitants are made members of the town.

Many of these sanctuaries represent monuments worthy of being protected for their artistic and historical value. Some of them, like the great mosques of the Qayrawānians (al-Qarawiyīn) and the Andalusians (al-'Andalūs),[1] and the *madāris* attached to them, count among the masterpieces of Maghribi art (or Hispano-Moorish, if one wishes and on condition of not forgetting that the Almohad and Almoravid empires had their center of gravity in Africa and not in Spain). Many other sanctuaries, which do not manifest the same originality of invention or the same splendor, nonetheless merit to be the object of attentive and effective protection on account of their beauty and because they bear witness to the perfect vitality of Moroccan art and its continuity throughout the centuries. The most modest sanctuaries are not necessarily the least valuable from this point of view: the simplicity and sobriety of their forms often creates an ambience of truth and peace.

All in all, what strikes the visitor of the numerous sanctuaries in Fez is not so much the diversity of the architectural types as their unity throughout the centuries. This unity in time, or this tradition, is explained above all by the conscious and consequent reference to a single model, that of the very first mosque established in the domestic courtyard of the Prophet in Medina. It is the peristyle mosque, common to the entire Arab world but developed with a particularly rigorous logic in the Maghrib: the prayer hall, whose horizontal roof is supported by pillars or arcades, opens on the opposite side of the *qiblah* (the direction of Mecca) onto a rectangular courtyard, which prolongs the prayer hall properly so-called and which is surrounded by porticos or galleries reminiscent of the *ṣuffah* (bench) where the poorest of the Prophet's companions found shelter. This courtyard normally contains a fountain, which is used for the ritual ablutions.

In most cases, the prayer hall extends more in width than in length, in keeping with the ordering of the faithful during the communal prayer. The nave, or naves, that form the prayer hall are then transversal in relation to the axis of the *qiblah*. This axis, which is already indicated by the *miḥrāb*, the prayer niche, is further emphasized by the symmetric ordering of the space, particularly by a sort of transept going from the courtyard to the *miḥrāb*. When the naves are longitudinal, one refers to a "central nave," which is often wider than the others. One or two domes, or even a series of them, located on the extremities of the central nave can enhance this part of the building. Sometimes also the axis of the *miḥrāb* is simply acknowledged by a greater amplitude of the arcades which in some way reflect the *miḥrāb* toward the courtyard. In the great mosques, the arcade located in the middle of the portico and giving onto the courtyard is closed off by a wooden screen, the *'anazah*, which serves, so to speak, as a "summer *miḥrāb*" for those who pray in the courtyard.

Let us note in passing, since we shall return to these elements of construction, that the naves are covered with wooden roofs, either flat and supporting terraces, or gabled and covered with green tiles. The columns supporting these roofs are directly linked by ceiling beams or else they form part of the arcades. The entrance is preferably located on the side of the courtyard, and the minaret rises by the entrance itself or by one of the corners of the building.

[1] So named because founded by immigrants from the Maghribi city of Qayrawān (Kairouan) in present-day Tunisia and from the region of Arab Andalusia in present-day Spain. —Editors' Note

These are the principal elements of the fundamental plan, to which accessory elements can be added: an *imām*'s room, a library (*khizānah*), a storage-place for the *minbar*, or an ablution room. These may be located inside or outside of the rectangle delineating both the prayer hall and the courtyard. Their arrangement within the overall plan can be the cause of serious difficulties when they encroach upon a space already limited by site constraints. In the small mosques and those built in the narrow passageway between pre-existing buildings, one finds all kinds of abbreviations or condensations of the fundamental approach.

Among the accessory elements located inside or outside of a mosque, the ablution room (*mīḍā'h*) includes a certain number of latrines and a basin of pure water where the faithful perform their ritual ablutions. The *mīḍā'h* is ventilated by a small inner courtyard or a roof lantern pierced by windows. When it is directly accessible from the street or is situated in front of the mosque, it inevitably makes up part of the neighborhood's sanitary facilities and requires special maintenance which is often lacking today.

To ensure a sufficient flow of water for the ablutions, mosques are often located nearby a branch of the *wādī*, upstream from the point where this branch starts to carry away the waste water. Some of the mosques are constructed on the river itself, others either by a spring whose water is captured in basins built into the mosque's foundation, or near to where a strong-flowing spring issues from a cave now incorporated into a home bordering the sanctuary. This is to say that the majority of the mosques of Fez are integrated into the hydraulic network of the Wādī al-Fās and undergo its vicissitudes.

We have already mentioned the relationship that exists between the neighborhood mosques and the Koranic schools (*msīd*), the latter being at times installed in the mosque itself, on a floor above the street. Often these mosques also house a series of shops in their outer walls, the rent from which helps to cover the cost of maintaining the sanctuary.

One should make a distinction between ordinary mosques and cathedral mosques which are used for Friday worship and have a *minbar*, a pulpit or cathedra. The rank of cathedral mosque is granted by the king. The sanctuaries of this grade are distributed in such a way that each of them can accommodate a portion of the city's inhabitants. Fifteen of these "Friday mosques" (*jawāmi'*, plural of *jāmi'*) can be counted at present in the Fez medina, three of which, al-Qarawiyīn, Mūlay Idrīs, and al-Dīwān, are located in the center relatively close to one another. The Qarawiyīn alone has a capacity of almost twenty thousand faithful, which makes one think that in the time when the ancient university-mosque flourished, the majority of the male inhabitants gathered there on Friday. The most spacious mosques, apart from al-Qarawiyīn and Mūlay Idrīs, are those of al-'Andalūs, Bāb al-Jīssah, and Ibn Junūd, located at the city's most important gates, together with the Raṣīf Mosque.

Certain neighborhood mosques are located on an intersecting "knot" of secondary streets, while others serve a more or less populous commercial sector, such as the markets which line the length of Tala'a al-Kabīra, Tala'a al-Ṣaghīra, Nakhīl, Saffāḥ, and Raṣīf. Moreover, it is a general characteristic of Muslim cities that the most important markets and the great sanctuaries are close to one another, a trait expressing the unity of the religious and social orders.

Not every mosque necessarily has a minaret, the call to prayer being made often from a terrace. By referring on a map to the location of all the functioning minarets and by tracing around each of them a circle whose radius corresponds to the reach of the muezzin's voice (approximately sixty-five meters), one obtains an almost total coverage of the urban space, with the exception of the areas formerly filled with orchards *intra muros*. That is to say that the urban fabric is measured by an acoustic unity, which is not at all surprising if one considers that the call announcing the various times for prayer essentially determines the rhythm of life in the medina.

Among the oldest mosques of Fez, some boast curious "hanging" (*mu'allaq*) prayer rooms constructed as a bridge-like passage (*sabāṭ*) over the street. These prayer rooms, which seem to be a specialty of Fez, may have a Saharan origin since popular tradition has them going back to the Almoravids. They corroborate, moreover, the often contested analogy between certain streets of Fez and those of the Saharan kasbahs with their superstructures interrupted by "light wells." Mosques of this type usually have their entrance as well as their ablution room on the ground floor; from there, a staircase leads to the prayer hall which is generally wider than the street and which connects to a terrace serving as a "summer prayer hall." Most of these mosques have their own minaret.

Most mosques containing tombs were first *zawāyā* (plural of *zāwiyah*), or still are so, as in the case of the cathedral mosque of S. Aḥmad ibn Nāṣir, which is in fact an extension of the Nāṣiriyyah *zāwiyah* of Fez. The tomb of the saint to whom the *zāwiyah* is dedicated is often found in a room opening onto the courtyard and facing the prayer hall. The place where the saint was buried is marked with a sort of wooden chest, covered with veils. The ceiling of the funerary room is frequently formed by a wooden dome which surrounds and protects a masonry construction, as in the *zāwiyah* of Mūlay Idrīs.

This is also the form of most of the independent mausoleums: they generally have a cubic base which carries either a wooden dome covered on the outside by a pyramidal roof with green tiles, or a hemispherical dome in brick. Mausoleums of this type dominate the numerous private cemeteries (*rawḍah*) in the city's outlying districts.

The decoration of the interior of the mosques and *zawāyā* of Fez is concentrated primarily on the prayer niche, the *miḥrāb*. Certain prayer niches are very simple and devoid of all ornament. In many cases, however, these niches are framed and crowned with a panel of arabesques and inscriptions in sculptured plaster whose shimmering relief and snow-like appearance contrasts with the black ceiling beams and with the sometimes rough appearance of the prayer hall. The more recent the stucco panel—and it can be very recent, since the art of sculptured plaster is still alive—the more it gives the impression of a piece of fabric or a veil applied to the wall. In relatively old pieces, the relief is more differentiated and more directly wraps around the arch of the niche, this arch taking on the form of a multi-contoured halo. One recognizes without difficulty that the model here is the *miḥrāb* of the Great Mosque of Córdoba, a model which the Great Mosque (*Jāmi' al-Kabīr*) of Fās al-Jādīd, of Marinid origin, retraces with much vigor. The three or five "blind" or stained glass windows which are aligned above the *miḥrāb* confirm this design's Córdoban filiation. In almost every case, moreover, the niche itself is pentagonal, like that of the celebrated *miḥrāb* of Córdoba.

In second place, the decoration of a mosque or *zāwiyah* relates to the paving of the courtyard. The latter is most often done in ceramic tiles (*zillīj*) up to the foot of the walls which are covered with mosaics of the same material. The great majority of the small mosques, however, have no wall decoration other than rush mats fixed onto the walls and pillars. As for the floor itself of the prayer hall, the ground is paved or rammed, then overlaid with fiber matting of dwarf palm. In the richer sanctuaries, the wall mosaics are framed with friezes of writing drawn on incised ceramic plaques.

The floor's decoration is matched by that of the ceiling, which can be made of simple horizontal beams, or, in more sophisticated buildings, of a three-sided cradle called a *birshlah*, whose cross-section resembles the letter A, the horizontal line corresponding to the top of the ceiling. In buildings with an octagonal base and wooden domes, the beams forming the facets of the domes intersect each other at the ridge to form a geometrical rosette. Sometimes also the domes are simply made by an assemblage of painted wooden strips, supported by beams secured in a brick superstructure.

More than anything else it is the form of the arcades measuring the interior space of the mosque which confers upon the latter its quality. In this respect it can be affirmed that the religious architecture of Fez has remained faithful to its Almohad heritage. The arcades' form has slightly evolved, becoming more pointed with a more pronounced rectangular framework, but nothing more.

On the exterior of a mosque, the object of special decoration is the main portal. It is often sheltered by a wooden awning covered in green tiles and supported by sculptured brackets setting off a plaster frieze.

The vast majority of sanctuaries are maintained thanks to the pious foundations (*aḥbās* or *awqāf*) which have been formed for this purpose and which consist of productive real properties such as fields, orchards, *fanādiq*, shops, rental houses, or bath houses (*ḥammāmāt*).

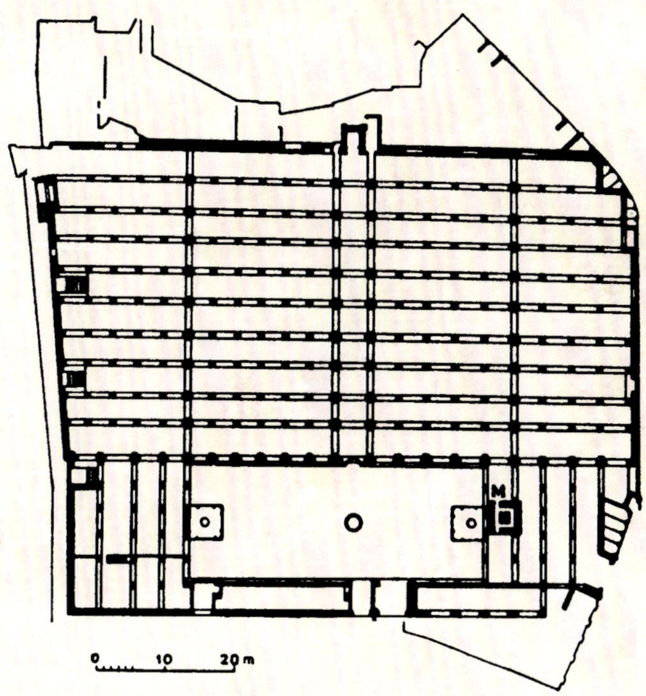

Plan of al-Qarawiyīn University-Mosque.
In the foreground is the courtyard with a fountain on each of its shorter sides and the minaret of the mosque on the right. The central nave of the great hall leads to the prayer-niche (*miḥrāb*). A subsidiary nave leads to an annex containing the library and the mosque used for funerals.

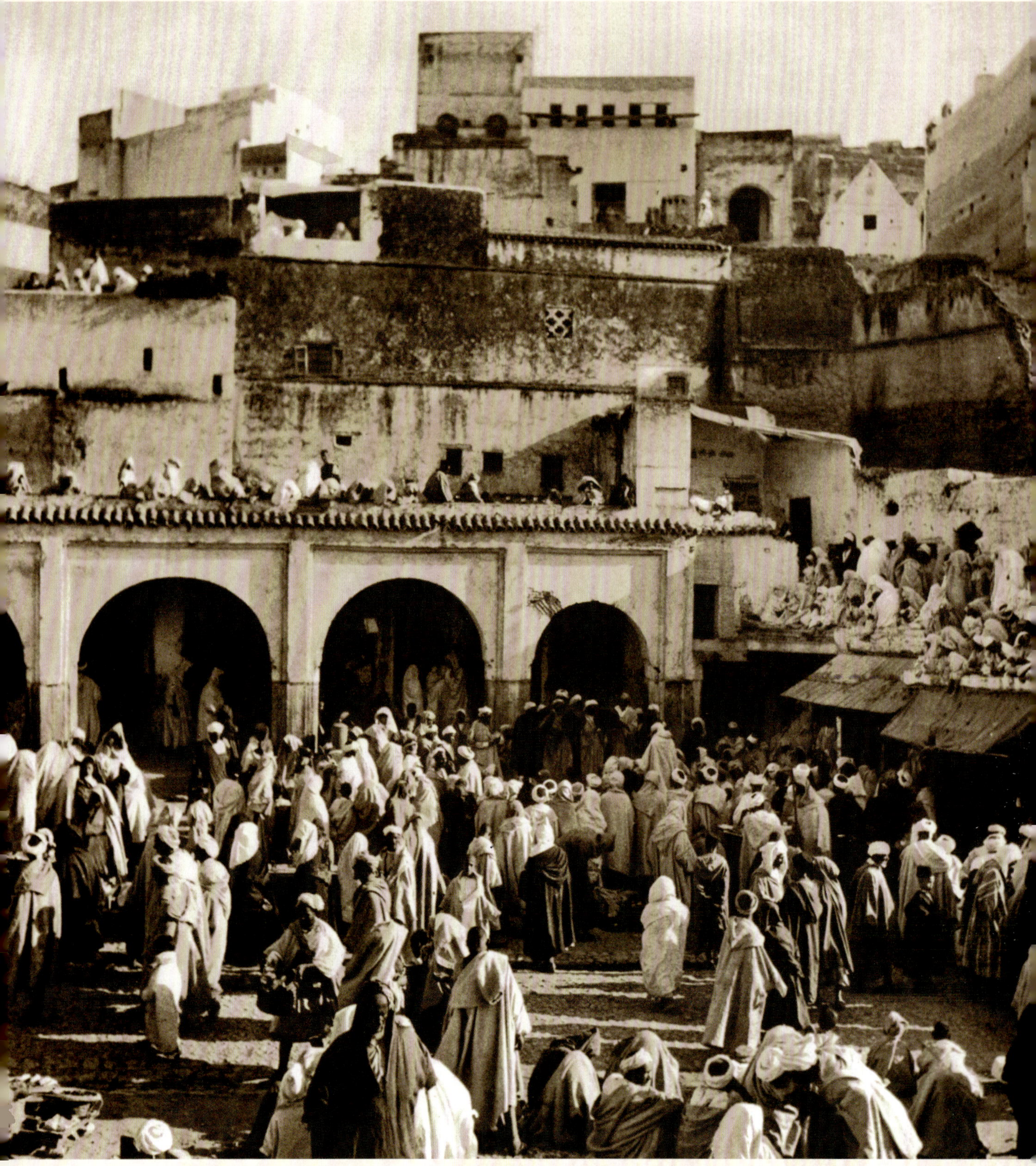

Marketplace in the town of Mūlay Idrīs during the annual festival in honor of this saint

Appendix II

Key Thoughts

Some Characteristic Traits of a Muslim City

1. In Islam there is no scission between the religious order and social order. Koranic law and Prophetic custom (*sunnah*) encompass both domains. As a result, the cultural or spiritual structure of a Muslim city and its material structure overlay one another.

2. The rhythm of urban life being determined by the times of prayer, the mosques with their minarets are located in such a way that the voice of the muezzin reaches every dwelling; hence the, so to say, acoustical layout of the town, one which is particularly evident in Fez.

3. In principle, every Muslim town is born of a marketplace located in the shadow of a sanctuary. The marketplace attracts the manual trades, while the sanctuary attracts the teaching of sacred sciences. The town center of Fez is a good example of the cohabitation of worship, learning, commerce, and art. The grouping of buildings corresponding to these various activities is apparent; it is even more so in certain Eastern cities.

4. Dwellings are separated as far as possible from these centers of public life, being sites where masculine activities take place. Houses are turned towards their inner courtyards and are generally reached at the end of blind alleyways. This order of things is particularly accentuated in Arabo-Islamic cities, with the exception of southern Arabia where "wind houses" prevail. The concentration of houses on an inner courtyard is nonetheless found from Iran to Afghanistan. In Muslim countries with colder climates, the house's intimacy is ensured by other arrangements, such as the use of gardens surrounded by high walls, notably in Turkey.

5. The choice of the site of a Muslim town primarily depends upon water resources, and this not only for cities located in relatively arid zones. Water is at once the guarantor of life, an element of religious purification, and a medium for pleasure. In the houses and streets of Fez, it is the fountains that are the object of the richest ornamentation.

6. According to the words of the Prophet, every Muslim is in principle secure in his person, his family, and his property; at the same time, he must efface himself in the community. Consequently, the best form for a town is the one which guarantees the greatest liberty in the private or familial domain, while ensuring a perfect coordination in the public domain.

7. The tendency to translate the Islamic community into solidarities of various levels: brotherhoods, guilds, neighborhood groups, etc.

8. Domestic life, even when it is refined, can at any moment be reduced to very simple forms, which correspond to the Prophetic custom; for example, communal meals taken seated on the floor.

9. The importance of the *awqāf* or pious foundations.

Some Permanent Values of the Traditional Urbanism of Fez

1. The profoundly human quality of the medina: there is a common measure between man, habitable room (*bayt*), house, neighborhood, and city. We can also say that everything in the medina is made to man's measure, hence the stimulating, reassuring, and humanly warm nature of the ambience. This is in contrast to the often inhuman ambience of modern cities.

2. The value accorded to familial and private life, which, thanks to the architecture of an inner courtyard, is protected not only from noise and dust, but also from the turmoil and coarseness of public life.

3. The organization of marketplaces and craft quarters following a guild model which favors social and professional solidarity. From the point of view of town-planning, the distribution of the markets is often perfect: consider, for example, the small market squares parallel to the Souk al-'Attārīn.

4. The coincidence, in architecture along with the crafts in general, of the useful and the beautiful, and consequently the absence of the modern dichotomy opposing skill and art.

5. The integration, both utilitarian and ornamental, of water into architecture, as well as the love of interior gardens.

6. The lack of any scission between religious and profane life.

7. The integration of tombs and cemeteries in daily life; the absence of a "fear of death."

8. The capacity of the Fāssī craftsman to adapt, notably his capacity to produce functional objects with a minimum of means, and consequently also in a minimal space.

The qualities listed under nos. 1-5 directly concern town-planning, the others refer to it indirectly. In all this one must not forget that an urban tradition such as the one we have examined has psychological and spiritual roots that are too profound for one to manipulate as one sees fit. However, it is always possible to identify essential elements susceptible of being transposed in a materially different context.

Craftsmanship: Authentic Expression of the Tradition

1. Definition of the craftsman: different from the artist? Traditionally no. Difference with industry: the craftsman creates unique objects, not repeated like those of the machine. He does not create arbitrarily but within the framework of a certain formal language having its own rules—its grammar, its syntax—which to contradict would produce not only dissonance but properly speaking non-sense.

2. The formal language of Moroccan craftsmanship: imprint of Islam, which is more than a religious sentiment and more than a philosophy, being a spiritual wisdom, a *ḥikmah*; then, imprint of the Moroccan ethnic character, of a "temperament," where Arab and Berber heredities converge.

The imprint of Islam: the reflection of divine Unity in the perfection of the object, perfection which is at once beauty—*jamāl*—and equilibrium, generosity and necessity, thus lack of arbitrariness. The ethnic imprint, in comparison with the art of other Islamic countries: a certain sense of the essential, a preference for purely geometric forms, a sobriety and virility, qualities which are at once Arab—in the original sense of the term—and Berber.

3. Situation of the Moroccan craftsman in the modern world: his enemy, industrialization; his advantage, his increasingly rare and unique nature.

Sources

Author's Preface: From "Alternatives fausses et réelles," a lecture given in 1976 to a group of Moroccan students visiting the Fez Master Plan Workshop; "Fès, une ville humain," a lecture given on April 21, 1973 to members of the Association for the Protection of Fez, published in *Études Traditionnelles*, July-September, no. 485 (1984) pp. 124-129; and "Fès et l'art de l'Islam," a lecture given on April 25, 1978 to students of the Mūlay Idrīs High School, published in *Actes du Séminaire expérimental d'animation culturelle* (Paris: UNESCO, 1980), vol. I, p. 12.

Chapter 1: From "Les constants de l'urbanisme arabo-musulman et l'example de Fès," a paper delivered between April 22-27, 1974 at a UNESCO sponsored colloquium held in Ḥammāmāt, Tunisia; "Project pour la réhabilitation du centre de la médina de Fès," a project prepared together with Stefano Bianca for the Fez Master Plan Workshop; "La médina de Fès—une forme de vie désuète?," a lecture given on April 12, 1974 to mark the launch of the Association for the Protection of Fez; "Fès hier, aujourd'hui, demain," a paper delivered between July 19-23, 1976 at a UNESCO sponsored colloquium held in Cambridge, England, published in *The Islamic City*, ed. R.B. Serjeant (Paris: UNESCO, 1980), pp. 166-176; and "Fès, une ville humain."

Chapter 2: From "Pour sauver la médina de Fès," a lecture given on February 17, 1973 to members of the Association for the Protection of Fez; "Pourquoi protéger l'architecture d'une ville comme l'ancienne Fès?," an undated lecture; "Fès, une ville humain"; "Les constants de l'urbanisme arabo-musulman"; and "La médina de Fès."

Chapter 3: From "Valeurs permanents de l'art maghrébin," a paper delivered on May 9, 1973 to alumni of the Mūlay Idrīs College; "La conception de la beauté dans l'art islamique," a lecture dated 1976; "Valeur et rang du patrimoine artistique de Fès," a project published in *Schéma directeur d'urbanisme de la ville de Fès* (Paris: UNESCO, 1980), vol. 2, pp. 29-30; and "Fès et l'Art de l'Islam."

Chapter 4: From "L'artisanat traditionnel au Maroc: sa nature et sa destinée," an undated lecture; "L'artisanat marocain: une chance!" an undated lecture; "L'artisanat, expression authentique de la tradition," a lecture given in December, 1972 to city officials of Meknes; "La médina de Fès"; "Fès hier, aujourd'hui, demain"; "Pourquoi protéger l'architecture?"; and "La conception de la beauté".

Appendix I: From "Introduction à l'inventaire des sanctuaries de la Médina," a project prepared for the Fez Master Plan Workshop.

Appendix II: From "Quelques traits caractéristiques de la ville musulmane en general et leur expression dans la forme spatial de Fès," an undated note; "Quelques valeurs permanents de l'urbanisme traditionnel de Fès," a note dated April 20, 1976; and "L'artisanat traditionnel au Maroc."

Glossary of Terms

'abd: servant.
adab: proper comportment; code of spiritual courtesy.
aḥbās: plural of *ḥubs*, a pious foundation.
'ajā'ib: curiosa; strange, unusual, or marvelous objects.
'ālim: learned scholar of Islam; expert in Islamic jurisprudence.
amīn: man of trust; the "provost" of a guild.
'anazah: wooden screen used as a removable *miḥrāb*.
aswāq: plural of *sūq*, a souk or marketplace.
awqāf: plural of *waqf*, a pious foundation; synonym of *ḥubs* (plural, *aḥbās*).
bāb: gate.
barakah: divine blessing; spiritual influx.
bay'ah: pact of fidelity to a leader.
bayt: habitable room.
birshlah: wooden ceiling beams arranged in the shape of an uppercase "A," the horizontal line corresponding to the top of ceiling.
burj: tower.
buyūt: plural of *bayt*, a habitable room.
caliphal: from caliph (*khalīfah*), representative (of God or His Prophet); politically, head of state.
cardo: in Roman cities a street oriented north-south.
corps de logis: the principal block of a large, usually classical, mansion or palace.
ḍarīḥ: mausoleum; synonym of *qabr*.
decumanus: in Roman cities a street oriented east-west.
fanādiq: plural of *funduq*, a combined hotel and warehouse.
Fāssī: relating to the city of Fez (Fās).
fiqh: law, jurisprudence in Islam.
funduq: combined hotel and warehouse; caravanserai.
genius loci: the distinctive atmosphere or pervading spirit of a place.
ḥadīth: collected sayings of the Prophet Muhammad.
ḥammāmāt: plural of *ḥammām*, a public bath house.
ḥammām: pubic bath house.
ḥaram: sanctuary; holy site.
ḥarām: forbidden; also sacred and inviolable.
Hijrah: in reference to the *hijrah* (journey) of the Prophet Muhammad from Mecca to Medina, marking the first year of the Islamic calendar (622 AD).
ḥikmah: wisdom.
ḥubs: pious foundation; synonym of *waqf* (plural, *awqāf*).
'ibād: plural of *'abd*, a servant.
iḥsān: beauty; also excellence or perfection.
imām: leader of the required daily prayer.
in potentia: potentially; as a possibility.
inshirāḥ: expansion; beatific dilation.
intra muros: within the (city) walls.
jamāl: beauty.
jāmi': assembly; a "cathedral mosque" used for Friday prayers.
jawāmi': plural of *jāmi'*, a "cathedral mosque."
jibs: sculptured stucco work.
kasbah: from *qaṣbah*, a fortress or walled city.
khizānah: library.
kulliyāt: architectural complex combining a mosque, college, royal mausoleum, etc.
Kūfic: style of calligraphy, named after the town of Kufāh in Iraq.
kursi'l-'ilm: teaching chair.
madāris: plural of *madrasah*, place of study; a college of religious instruction.
Maghrib: west; the western part of the Islamic world, i.e., north-west Africa and

Spain.
Maghribi: relating to the Maghrib, the western part of the Islamic world.
maḥkamah: courthouse.
mahārib: plural of *miḥrāb*, the prayer niche indicating the direction of prayer.
masjid: mosque.
mellah: from *millāḥ*, a Moroccan city's Jewish quarter and also banking quarter.
mīḍā'h: ablution room.
miḥrāb: prayer niche indicating the direction of prayer (*qiblah*).
minbar: pulpit or cathedra.
msīd: Koranic school.
muḥtasib: inspector of all markets, controlling the quality of goods and their prices.
mu'allaq: hanging; hanging prayer room constructed as a bridge-like passage (*sabāṭ*) over a street.
mu'allim: master craftsman.
mukhfiyyah: hidden.
qabr: mausoleum; synonym of *ḍarīḥ*.
qīsāriyyah: central marketplace for precious objects, e.g., fine textiles and jewels.
qiblah: the direction for prayer, towards Mecca.
qwādsiyah: sewage workers.
rawḍah: garden; also cemetery.
riyāḍ: enclosed garden.
sabab: secondary or occasional cause.
sabāṭ: enclosed bridge-like passage over a street.
ṣaḥn: the large courtyard of a mosque.
ṣāni': artist; also craftsman.
Sharīfian: relating to a *sharīf*, a descendant of the Prophet.
sīrah: journey; life-story (of the Prophet).
ṣuffah: raised seating-area in the first mosque made for the poor to rest.
sunnah: wont; the model established by the Prophet Muhammad, as transmitted in the *ḥadīth*.
sūq: plural, *aswāq*, souk, bazaars, or marketplace.
sūrah: chapter of the Koran.
Taifas: from *ṭā'ifah*, one of several competing principalities that arose in Muslim Spain after the collapse of the Umayyad Caliphate.
taṣawwuf: Sufism; the interior or mystical dimension of Islam.
tawḥīd: assertion or recognition of the divine Oneness, which is the cardinal Islamic doctrine.
ṭullāb: plural of *ṭulba*, student.
'ulamā': plural of *'ālim*, learned scholar of Islam.
'umanā': plural of *amīn*, man of trust.
'urf: customary law.
wādī: valley; in the Maghrib, used to refer to a river (elsewhere, a dry riverbed).
waqf: pious foundation; synonym of *ḥubs* (plural, *aḥbās*).
zawāyā: plural of *zāwiyah*, a meeting place of a Sufi order.
zāwiyah: literally "corner"; a meeting place of a Sufi order.
zillīj: mosaic work of enameled faience.
zillayji: mosaic worker.

For a glossary of all key foreign words used in books published by World Wisdom, including metaphysical terms in English, consult: www.DictionaryofSpiritualTerms.org. This on-line Dictionary of Spiritual Terms provides extensive definitions, examples and related terms in other languages.

List of Illustrations

All photographs and sketches are by the author, unless noted by an asterisk (*)

Index of People, Places, and Terms

Biographical Notes

Titus Burckhardt, a German Swiss, was born in Florence in 1908 and died in Lausanne in 1984. He devoted all his life to the study and exposition of the different aspects of wisdom and tradition. In the age of modern science and technocracy, Titus Burckhardt was one of the most remarkable of the exponents of universal truth, in the realm of metaphysics as well as in the realm of cosmology and of traditional art. He was a major voice of the *philosophia perennis*, that "wisdom uncreate" that is expressed in Platonism, Vedanta, Sufism, Taoism, and other authentic esoteric or sapiential teachings. In literary and philosophic terms, he was an eminent member of the "Traditionalist" or "Perennialist" school of twentieth century thinkers and writers. Titus Burckhardt was also an expert on Islam, Islamic arts and crafts, and its spiritual dimension, Sufism.

Although Burckhardt was born in Florence, he was the scion of a patrician family of Basle, Switzerland. He was the great-nephew of the famous art-historian Jacob Burckhardt and the son of the sculptor Carl Burckhardt.

Burckhardt lived for many years in Fez, Morocco and was an integral part of the Moroccan government's successful preservation of the ancient medina of Fez as a UNESCO World Heritage Site in 1981. Burckhardt's work has also provided a blueprint for the preservation of other Islamic cities of great historical interest. In 1999 the Moroccan government sponsored an international symposium in Marrakesh in honor of Burckhardt's work entitled, "Sagesse et Splendeur des Arts islamiques—Hommage à Titus Burckhardt". The proceedings were published with the financial assistance of UNESCO in 2000.

Burckhardt was also a senior consultant for over a decade to Skidmore, Owings & Merrill (founded in 1936), one of the world's leading architecture, urban design, engineering, and interior architecture firms, with projects in more than fifty countries. In that capacity he was a major factor in the preservation of architectural sites of immense historical importance in many Islamic countries.

Burckhardt was fluent in German, French, Arabic, and English and wrote seventeen books in German, eight books in French, translated three books from Arabic into French, and wrote numerous articles in various languages. Fifteen of his books have been translated and published in English.

Jean-Louis Michon, born in Nancy, France in 1924, was a traditionalist writer, editor, translator, Arabist, and artistic consultant who specialized in Islam in North Africa, Islamic art, and Sufism. After a time spent teaching high school in Damascus, Syria, he obtained a Ph.D. in Islamic studies at Paris University (Sorbonne). From 1972 to 1980, Michon was Chief Technical Adviser to a series of joint programs by UNESCO, the UN Development Program, and the Moroccan government aimed at the preservation of traditional arts and crafts. His mission coincided in time with the one entrusted to his friend Titus Burckhardt for the preservation of the old city of Fez. Michon was the author of *Autobiography* (*Fahrasa*) *of a Moroccan Sufi: Ahmad*

Ibn 'Ajiba and *Introduction to Traditional Islam, Illustrated: Foundations, Art, and Spirituality*. He was also co-editor (with Roger Gaetani) of *Sufism: Love & Wisdom*. He died in 2013 in Lausanne, Switzerland, where he had lived since 1952.

Joseph A. Fitzgerald studied Comparative Religion at Indiana University, where he also earned a Doctor of Jurisprudence degree. He is an award-winning editor whose previous publications include *Honen the Buddhist Saint: Essential Writings and Official Biography*; *The Way and the Mountain: Tibet, Buddhism, and Tradition*; *The Essential Sri Anandamayi Ma: Life and Teachings of a 20th Century Saint from India*; *An Illustrated Introduction to Taoism: The Wisdom of the Sages*; *Of the Land and the Spirit: The Essential Lord Northbourne on Ecology and Religion* (with Christopher James); *A Christian Woman's Secret: A Modern-Day Journey to God*; *The Cheyenne Indians: Their History and Lifeways*; *The Wisdom of Ananda Coomaraswamy: Reflections on Indian Art, Life, and Religion* (with S.D.R. Singam); *The Original Gospel of Ramakrishna: Based on M.'s English Text, Abridged*; *Spirit of the Earth: Indian Voices on Nature*; and *Spirit of the Indian Warrior*.

Jane Casewit is an educator, translator, and writer with a deep interest in religious education, religious studies, interfaith understanding, and metaphysics. She has many years of teaching experience in North Africa and the Middle East and held key positions in girls' education and community mobilization projects in that region as well as consulting in sub-Saharan Africa. In Morocco she worked for the United States Agency for International Development as an education and workforce development advisor. She edited *Education in the Light of Tradition: Studies in Comparative Religion*, translated *A Spirit of Tolerance: The Inspiring Life of Tierno Bokar*, and has written extensively on Islam and femininity. She presently designs education and workforce training programs for North Africa and the Middle East.

World Wisdom Titles by Titus Burckhardt

Art of Islam: Language and Meaning, Commemorative Edition, 2009

Chartres and the Birth of the Cathedral: Revised, 2010

The Essential Titus Burckhardt: Reflections on Sacred Art, Faiths, and Civilizations
edited by William Stoddart, 2003

The Foundations of Christian Art,
edited by Michael Oren Fitzgerald, 2006

Foundations of Oriental Art & Symbolism,
edited by Michael Oren Fitzgerald, 2009

Introduction to Sufi Doctrine, 2008

A Living Islamic City: Fez and Its Preservation,
edited by Jean-Louis Michon & Joseph A. Fitzgerald, 2020

Sacred Art in East and West: Its Principles and Methods, 2001

Siena: City of the Virgin, Illustrated, 2008

Titles on Islam by World Wisdom

Art of Islam, Language and Meaning: Commemorative Edition,
by Titus Burckhardt, 2009

Christianity/Islam: Perspectives on Esoteric Ecumenism,
by Frithjof Schuon, 2008

Emir Abd el-Kader: Hero and Saint of Islam,
by Ahmed Bouyerdene, 2012

Introduction to Sufi Doctrine,
by Titus Burckhardt, 2008

Introduction to Sufism: The Inner Path of Islam,
by Éric Geoffroy, 2010

Introduction to Traditional Islam, Illustrated: Foundations, Art, and Spirituality,
by Jean-Louis Michon, 2008

Islam, Fundamentalism, and the Betrayal of Tradition: Essays by Western Muslim Scholars,
edited by Joseph E.B. Lumbard, 2004

A Living Islamic City: Fez and Its Preservation,
by Titus Burckhardt, edited by Jean-Louis Michon & Joseph A. Fitzgerald, 2020

Maintaining the Sacred Center: The Bosnian City of Stolac,
by Rusmir Mahmutćehajić, 2011

Men of a Single Book: Fundamentalism in Islam, Christianity, and Modern Thought,
by Mateus Soares de Azevedo, 2010

The Mystics of Islam,
by Reynold A. Nicholson, 2002

Outline of Sufism: The Essentials of Islamic Spirituality,
by William Stoddart, 2012

The Path of Muhammad: A Book on Islamic Morals and Ethics by Imam Birgivi,
interpreted by Shaykh Tosun Bayrak, 2005

Paths to the Heart: Sufism and the Christian East,
edited by James S. Cutsinger, 2003

Paths to Transcendence: According to Shankara, Ibn Arabi, and Meister Eckhart,
by Reza Shah-Kazemi, 2006

The Philosophy of Ecstasy: Rumi and the Sufi Tradition,
edited by Leonard Lewisohn, 2015

The Sacred Foundations of Justice in Islam: The Teachings of 'Ali ibn Abi Talib,
edited by M. Ali Lakhani, 2006

A Spirit of Tolerance: The Inspiring Life of Tierno Bokar,
by Amadou Hampaté Bâ, 2008

The Sufi Doctrine of Rumi: Illustrated Edition
by William C. Chittick, 2005

Sufism: Love and Wisdom,
edited by Jean-Louis Michon and Roger Gaetani, 2006

Sufism: Veil and Quintessence,
by Frithjof Schuon, 2007

Symbol of Divine Light: The Lamp in Islamic Culture and Other Traditions
by Nicholas Stone, 2018

A Treasury of Sufi Wisdom: The Path of Unity,
by Peter Samsel, 2016

Understanding Islam,
by Frithjof Schuon, 2011

Universal Dimensions of Islam: Studies in Comparative Religion,
edited by Patrick Laude, 2010

The Universal Spirit of Islam: From the Koran and Hadith,
edited by Judith and Michael Oren Fitzgerald, 2006

Unveiling the Garden of Love: Mystical Symbolism in Layla Majnun and Gita Govinda,
by Lalita Sinha, 2008

What Does Islam Mean in Today's World: Religion, Politics, Spirituality,
by William Stoddart, 2012

Wisdom's Journey: Living the Spirit of Islam in the Modern World,
by John Herlihy, 2009

Titles in the Sacred Art in Tradition Series

Art from the Sacred to the Profane: East and West,
by Frithjof Schuon, edited by Catherine Schuon, 2007

Art of Islam: Language and Meaning, Commemorative Edition,
by Titus Burckhardt, 2009

Chartres and the Birth of the Cathedral: Revised,
by Titus Burckhardt, 2010

The Foundations of Christian Art,
by Titus Burckhardt, edited by Michael Oren Fitzgerald, 2006

Foundations of Oriental Art & Symbolism,
by Titus Burckhardt, edited by Michael Oren Fitzgerald, 2009

A Living Islamic City: Fez and Its Preservation,
by Titus Burckhardt, edited by Jean-Louis Michon & Joseph A. Fitzgerald, 2020

Sacred Art in East and West: Its Principles and Methods,
by Titus Burckhardt, 2001

Siena: City of the Virgin, Illustrated,
by Titus Burckhardt, 2008

Symbol of Divine Light: The Lamp in Islamic Culture and Other Traditions,
by Nicholas Stone, 2018